PRAISE FOR COMMANDO DAD: BASIC TRAINING:

'One of the best parenting books I've ever read'
Lorraine Kelly

'brilliant book'
The Daily Telegraph

'The advice, approved by healthcare professionals, is quick to read, easy
to understand and simple to digest, delivered in short, unambiguous
bullet points and, no-nonsense rules – and, pretty unarguably, spot on'
Jon Henley, *The Guardian*

'A no-nonsense guide to being an elite dad or carer,
from birth to three years – great package'
The Bookseller

'A must-have for new dads
MADE Magazine

'Neil Sinclair experienced many life and death situations during his
six years as an Army Commando. But forget tracking drug traffickers
through the jungles of Belize or clearing mines in Iraq while dodging
sniper fire – the most daunting thing the dad of three has ever
faced is bringing his newborn son, Samuel, home from hospital'
Baby & Me magazine

Vie Books is an imprint of Summersdale Publishers Ltd

Summersdale Publishers Ltd
46 West Street
Chichester
West Sussex
PO19 1RP
UK

www.summersdale.com

Printed and bound in the Czech Republic

ISBN: 978-1-84953-884-8

Substantial discounts on bulk quantities of Summersdale books are available to corporations, professional associations and other organisations. For details contact Nicky Douglas by telephone: +44 (0) 1243 756902, fax: +44 (0) 1243 786300 or email: nicky@summersdale.com.

DISCLAIMER
Neither the authors nor the publisher can be held responsible for any loss or claim arising out of the use, or misuse, of the suggestions made herein. Laws and regulations do change, so the reader should seek up-to-date professional advice on such issues. *Commando Dad: Mission Adventure* should not be considered as a substitute for your own common sense.

COMMANDO DAD

MISSION ADVENTURE

GET ACTIVE WITH YOUR KIDS

NEIL SINCLAIR

vie

ABOUT THE AUTHOR

Neil Sinclair is an ex-commando, qualified childminder and full-time dad to three young troopers! He is the author of the bestselling parenting guide *Commando Dad: Basic Training* (ISBN: 978 1 84953 261 7). He lives in Derbyshire.

CONTENTS

FOREWORD

Samuel Sinclair, 14

My dad asked me if I wanted to write a few lines about the adventures we'd had for this book. I did. When I think of the experiences that I have shared with him, my brother, my sister and my mum, my feelings can only be described in one word: privileged. When I was younger I don't think I realised how lucky I was. People are always asking my dad when he is writing a book for teenagers, so I think now I am giving him something back. Haha ☺

Jude Sinclair, 13

As my siblings and I get older, we start to spend less and less time with our parents, and more with our friends. It happens to all of us. But the time you spend with your parents is so precious. I have just turned 13, and my love for my mum and dad never ceases to amaze me. This book will definitely give you some insightful ideas about how you can make the best of the short time you have with your child. I've been told many times by my parents that to them it feels like just last week they were cradling me in their arms. And in another 13 years, who knows what we'll be doing. That's the fun part. You will share new experiences with your child every day even as they grow up. And that's what really matters.

Liberty Sinclair, 9

My mum and dad take me on lots of adventures. It's so fun! Going to the park is my favourite. I love climbing so climbing trees and monkey bars are best for me. I love it so much I climb at a club now! Whatever your child loves to do outside, try and make it possible for them. Staying fit and healthy is one of the most important things in life. My mum and dad are the best parents ever because they put so much time and effort into keeping me outside and active but happy at the same time. Thank you so much for reading my advice. Bye x

AUTHOR'S NOTE

I am a stay-at-home Commando Dad, and throughout my troopers' childhood I have personally tried and tested all of the activities in this book. I hope you find these activities useful and they inspire you to create your own adventures. If you want to share your ideas and thoughts with other Commando Dads, please share them on the *Commando Dad* website: www.commandodad.com/forum/

DEDICATION

To my unit: to my wife, Tara – thank you as ever for all of your help and support. To my own troopers, Sam, Jude and Liberty – writing this book has reminded me of the wonderful times we spent adventuring together. Thanks for the memories, and I'm looking forward to making more in the years to come.

INTRODUCTION

To all dads, carers and fellow adventurers: this book is for YOU.

You need to look lively, lads. Remember what it felt like to be a child, when you anticipated adventure around every corner? The excitement you felt when you woke up to find snow had fallen overnight? Or discovered an empty swing? The accomplishment of building a den? What happened? You grew up.

And that is what is happening to your own little troopers. Right now. In fact, less than 7,000 days from birth, they'll be 18 and making their own way in the world.

Which brings me to the first rule of Mission Adventure:

ACTING GROWN-UP IS NOT APPROPRIATE IN ALL SITUATIONS

Obviously, you need to be a responsible adult when it comes to the safety, health and well-being of both yourself and your unit. And to live in the modern world you will have to be grown-up in virtually all situations. But not every situation. I am calling upon you to recapture your inner adventurer. Because if you can teach your troopers that life can be full of fun and adventure – even as an adult – then you'll not only be entertaining them while building a whole host of important skills such as communication, creativity, cooperation and teamwork, but also giving them the means to a more fulfilling future. Because play and adventure isn't just for troopers – it's a key stress reliever and bonding activity for adults too.

When I was a commando in Operation Desert Storm my buddy and I came under sniper fire at a water point. Luckily, we were unharmed. We didn't go back to camp and wallow about what could have happened – we went back to be the butt of all the jokes about coming under fire from the worst shot in Iraq. In doing so, we were able to laugh about it – rid ourselves of the stress and anxiety and get up the next day and do our jobs effectively.

If all of the above weren't enough of a reason, then consider this: you are setting the stage for the next generation of Commando Dads (and Mums).

Now when I say 'adventure' I don't mean you have to climb the Eiger (I have. I wouldn't recommend it as a first activity). Adventure doesn't necessarily require spending money (most of the activities in this book cost nothing but time) or having special equipment. Adventure can be found in the everyday. You can make the walk to school a spy mission or Follow My Leader. And don't forget that childhood presents a lot of opportunities for your troopers to do things for the first time, which can be an adventure in itself: riding a bike, swimming, watching live sport (even better if their Commando Dad is taking part!) or live music, paddling in the sea or catching a train, to name but a few.

But you can also create more traditional adventures, from building a den, to making a fire, to exploring rock pools. These adventures can help your troopers to experience risk (albeit in a safe environment with you in charge) and in so doing to build their self-confidence and independence. But first:

YOU NEED TO FILL YOUR ADVENTURE ARMOURY

And this book can help. It's filled with good ideas and tips and tricks about how to entertain and adventure with your troopers. I've tested them in the field with my own three, and also as a teacher and childminder. They were a forgiving audience, and your troopers will be too. In fact, when it comes to having 'successful' adventures, the only thing you need to remember is to make sure you're engaged and doing it with them, and that your focus stays on the task in hand. You are their hero. If you engage with them, you will enhance the most everyday tasks into amazing adventures. You cannot fail.

Now, I live in the same busy world as you and know how hard it can be to block out all distractions, but I promise you that if you can carve out real time to be with your troopers it will pay dividends, because:

THE MOST EFFECTIVE TOOL IN YOUR ADVENTURE ARMOURY IS YOUR UNDIVIDED ATTENTION

That's not to say there won't be the inevitable setbacks and occasional failures with your adventures, of course – from not being able to control the weather, to not having what you need when you need it, and everything in between. But these will provide you with a golden opportunity to show your troopers how to deal with disappointment. They need to know that failure is a key element of success at any endeavour – imagine if the first time they had fallen over they decided to abandon learning to walk! Encourage and help them with a challenging task, but don't do it for them. Let them experience the challenge, and how sweet it feels to finally conquer something that was once too difficult. It will help them build resilience, a very valuable skill for them to carry into adulthood.

The fact is, you only have a short time with your trooper – you owe it to both of you to make as many of those days as adventurous and fun as possible. Think of this as an opportunity to relive your own childhood (or in some cases, create the one you wish you'd had). Only this time it will be better, because you are in charge.

Let the adventures begin!

HOW TO USE COMMANDO DAD: MISSION ADVENTURE

This book is designed to be used by dads 'in the field' when you are actively engaged in adventuring with your Junior Troopers (JT – approx. 5–9 years) and your Advanced Troopers (AT – approx. 9–12 years), and I have done my best to include a wide range of activities suitable for troopers of primary school age (5–12). However, you know the interests and abilities of your troopers and may find that some of these are suitable for adventurers outside of this age range. Just remember to employ your Commando Dad common sense to keep your troopers engaged – and safe.

This book isn't intended as a guide to every adventure you can have with your troops, but rather a few ideas to get you started. Every adventure comes with a mission brief to summarise the activity, mission key, indicating difficulty (boot symbol), expense (pound symbol) and suitability (Junior Trooper, etc.). There is also a kit list to show what you need and a 'Mission Accomplished' section where there's an opportunity for your trooper to put their signature. Gentlemen, I urge you to complete as many of these as you can as troopers grow up so, so quickly. Trust me when I tell you, you'll be glad to have kept a small record of your adventures together in future years.

Throughout the book I mention videos that demonstrate practical activities (such as tying knots) and you will find these on the Commando Dad website: www.commandodad.com. You'll also find forums on there and please do share your good ideas for trooper adventures with me – and other Commando Dads – on the forum pages.

Occasionally I use military terminology adapted for a parenting context, and to this end I have included a short glossary at the back of the book.

Your trooper's Basic Mission Adventure Kit

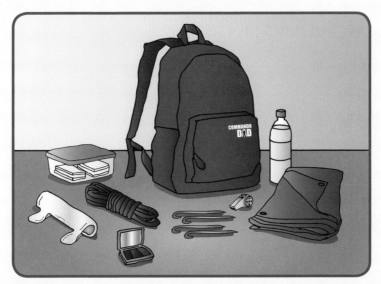

It isn't essential that you have a Basic Mission Adventure Kit for your trooper, but I found my troopers loved to take their little kitbags out and about on our missions.

Below is a list of suggested items.

Feel free to let them add or remove items depending on what mission you're planning with your unit. (However, remind your troopers not to pack too much. A heavy pack can become a real pain in the back.)

- Mission adventure backpack (30 cm x 30 cm x 10 cm) – approx. 10 litres capacity.
- Personal paracord (15 m).
- Personal tarpaulin (180 cm x 240 cm).
- Steel pegs x 8 (19 cm).
- 'Cam cream' (camouflage cream) for concealment purposes.
- Whistle with compass.
- Water bottle.
- Snack container.
- Empty plastic carrier bag (multiple uses).

Commando Dad's Basic Mission Adventure Kit

Whenever you adventure away from base camp, it's a good idea to have your Commando Dad Basic Mission Adventure Kitbag up to speed and squared away.

Below is a list of the contents you may consider. Amend it according to the mission, and the number of troopers you have under your command.

- **Kit list:** make sure you mentally (or physically) tick off each piece of required kit you need for your planned mission. Planning and preparation prevents poor parental performance – you don't want to get to your objective only to find you have left an essential piece of kit back at base camp.

- **Suitable clothing:** pack items appropriate to both the mission and the forecast. This could include waterproof tops and bottoms, gloves, hats, and sunscreen and lip balm.

- **Snacks and water.**

- **Pocketknife:** if appropriate for the mission, make sure you refer to the 'Knives and the Law' information in the Useful Resources section at the back of the book.

- **Sanitation protection:** wet wipes, hand sanitiser and plastic bags (for rubbish, wet garments, sitting on, etc.).

- **Waterproof notebook and pencils.**

- **Fully charged mobile phone:** just in case you need to call for backup support when out on manoeuvres.

- **First-aid kit:**

  ○ Sachets of paediatric paracetamol and paediatric ibuprofen. Check the label to ensure your trooper meets the weight and age requirements before administering.

  ○ A selection of plasters. Depending on the age of your trooper, make these bright and colourful as it can have a miraculous effect on the recovery process.

  ○ Finger bandage.

- ○ Antiseptic cream, also suitable for stings and bites.
- ○ Antiseptic wipes.
- ○ Tweezers, useful for removing splinters, etc.
- ○ Scissors, useful for cutting plasters, bandages, paracord, etc.

Useful additions to the first-aid kit (can be bought as and when you need them):

- Instant cold pack, to cool off bumps and bruises that your troopers may sustain during adventures.
- Saline solution and eye bath, just in case your troopers get any dust or grit in their eyes.

SECTION 1:

ADVENTURES IN BASE CAMP

CHAPTER 1:
MISSIONS IN BASE CAMP

MISSION 1:

BUILD AN INDOOR CAMP

Mission brief

- **Ground:** a 'low traffic' area in your base camp.
- **Situation:** enough clear floor space to create a den.
- **Mission:** to build, furnish and adventure in an indoor camp.
- **Time:** allow at least 30 minutes to erect your den.

KIT LIST:

- Your 'tent': sheets, tablecloths, towels, blankets.
- Support: the back of the sofa, armchairs, a table.
- Something heavy to anchor the tent if needed: door stops, books, cans of food, etc.
- Camp beds: pillows, duvets, blankets, sleeping bags.
- Activities: phone/camera for photos, radio, books, walkie-talkies, comics.

- Ration packs: prepared beforehand. Think healthy and non-staining: bottles of water, carrot batons, grapes, pretzels, oatcakes, crisps. If making sandwiches, use fillings like ham and cheese. Avoid fillings that make a mess (such as jam, chocolate spread or grated cheese).
- Light source: torches or electric candles if you have them.

*Good activity when entertaining troopers
from other units.*

INSTRUCTIONS:

1 **Secure your kit** by deploying your troopers throughout base camp. Give each trooper a short list of kit to find for the den. This should help avoid a squabbling squaddies situation.

2 **Build your camp** based on your resources and troopers. Be aware that the younger your trooper the more impatient they will be to complete the building stage. Alter your design accordingly. A fail-safe is a couple of sheets over a dining table, or a sheet over the back of a sofa.

3 **Give every trooper a task**, even if it is to take off cushion covers, get more supplies, or make a name card for the camp. Get creative.

4 When you have a suitable den, climb inside and **make any necessary adjustments**.

5 **Have an age-appropriate activity or two ready**, especially one where you can all take turns as this adds to the camaraderie you've created through building a camp together. Popular ones in my base camp include stories about ghosts and monsters, and the sticky note game, where you each have a sticky note on your head with a name on and you have to guess who you are by asking questions that require yes/no answers. Instead of a famous person, we use family members and friends. Your troopers are more likely to know the level of detail to ask questions and you'll be surprised what you'll find out about how your troopers see the world.

6 You may not want to stay in the camp all the time, preferring to let your older troopers have **independent play** – but they'll love that you all piled in at the start. Stay nearby, perhaps keeping guard at the perimeter of the camp.

7 **Tidy up.** When it's time to put the camp away, all troopers must help.

THE DEN COMMANDMENTS

Do:

- Let the troopers join in and listen to their suggestions. Trial and error is a great teacher.
- Use items that are ready for the wash to cut down on admin.
- Allow ration packs to be eaten in the camp.
- Arrange sorties around the house if your troops are older.

Don't:

- Take anything flammable or sharp into the camp.
- Have anything heavy anchoring the camp from above, in case it falls onto the occupants.
- Involve anything fragile. Anywhere.
- Have too many troopers in the den at once. There's always a rebellion.

MISSION ACCOMPLISHED

I verify that on this date .... I built and adventured in a camp with my Commando Dad.

Signed: ....

TARGET ACQUISITION
(TROOPER TREASURE HUNT)

Mission brief
- **Ground:** all over base camp and outside.
- **Situation:** works best when there are fewer people in the house, as this saves innocent victims getting caught in the crossfire.
- **Mission:** to solve the clues to find the target.
- **Time:** a good rule of thumb is to allow 10 minutes to find each target.

MISSION KEY

£ £ £ £ £   JT AT

KIT LIST:

- The target (or treasure) you need the troops to track down. This will depend on their age, but good ones that have worked for me in the past include:
  - Tickets. It's a good way to ramp up the excitement for a treat you have already planned.
  - Something related to a hobby they have, especially a collectable item.
  - Books/story CDs (you can get these from the library).
  - Christmas decorations.
  - Easter eggs (at Easter, of course).

- Costumes and props if you want the troops to dress up. If they are in the dress-up phase, go for it. If not, don't. You'll make the troopers feel awkward. Unsurprisingly, I always wanted to play as a soldier, but we've played this as fish, policemen, superheroes, royalty and cartoon characters.

- Clues, and give yourself enough time to think of good ones.

INSTRUCTIONS:

1 **Make your clues.** You can do this on paper slips that you hide, or actually directly onto something. This works on cereal boxes, empty loo rolls, fridges (using fridge magnets), magazines, mirrors (troops have to breathe on them to reveal the clue) and chalk on outdoor paving slabs. Obviously, the complexity of the clues you use will depend on the abilities of your troopers.

- For older troopers, you could write a message that needs to be held to a mirror to be read; or use invisible ink (*see 'Mission 13: Make Invisible Ink' in Missions in the Cookhouse*) that they'll need to paint over or heat with a hairdryer.
- For younger troopers, pictures or rhyming clues work well.
- Photographs make good clues (you can show these on an electronic device) especially when taken at close range, or from unusual angles.

2 **Include skills your trooper has learned,** like using a compass to find a clue due north (*see 'Mission: 32: Read a compass' in Missions in Wide Open Spaces*) or telling the time.

3 **Include as much physical activity as you can**, especially if you have outside space. Space the clues far apart; get the troops to climb a tree, commando crawl under a net, etc.

4 **Make up rules** and ensure that your game makes it easy for your troopers to stick to them. For example, it's no use deciding that running up and down the stairs is not acceptable if the clue that follows the one hidden in the bedroom is on the ground floor. Don't forget your Trooper Boundary Brief – i.e. to tell your troopers the places that are out of bounds during the game, such as kitchen cupboards, the fridge, the garage, etc.

5 **Make sure everyone knows the rules before you begin**. A good way to do this is for you to ask the troops to repeat a rule or two back to you. Listening, understanding and adhering to rules will be critical for the success of other adventures, and will keep troopers safe.

6 **Be flexible.** You may need to help the troops get some clues, they might find them in the wrong order, some clues may fail (like the time I put one in the paddling pool in a clear plastic folder and it got waterlogged and sank). The end game is for everyone to have fun, so keep that at the front of your mind.

7 **Tidy up.** When the game's over, deploy your troopers over base camp to tidy up.

If you have older troopers, they can help you devise the game and make the clues for the younger ones.

GOLDEN RULES

Do:

- Give the easiest clue first as this will help everyone get engaged with the game.
- Be creative. If the clues are too easy to find, the game will be over too soon. Good places include under shoes, folded inside the paper on a loo roll, inside money boxes, between the pages of books, taped to the inside door of cupboards.
- Get troopers to read out clues.
- Make sure that if there is a prize at the end of the hunt, you have enough so it can be shared out to all the hunting troopers.

Don't:

- Have too many children taking part. If you have no choice, split the troopers into groups to encourage teamwork, and to avoid a possible squabbling squaddies situation.
- Have too many clues, especially for younger troopers. You'll find the right number, but eight always works for me.

MISSION ACCOMPLISHED

I verify that on this date .... I hunted and acquired my target with my Commando Dad.

Signed: ....

LEARN TO TIE KNOTS

Mission brief

- **Ground:** make a template to enable you to practise anywhere (*see 'Mission 44: Make a template for tying knots' in Adventures in the Making*).
- **Situation:** no special situation required.
- **Mission:** to learn how to tie – and use – four important knots.
- **Time:** troopers can practise for hours.

MISSION KEY

£ £ £ £ £   JT   AT

KIT LIST:

- Several lengths of cord or thin rope.

For videos on how to tie the knots in this section, go to the 'Mission Adventure' section at www.commandodad.com.

Notes

Four very useful knots for your troopers to learn are:

- The overhand or thumb knot.
- The figure-of-eight knot.
- The square or reef knot.
- The bowline.

The very first step is to understand the anatomy of the rope:

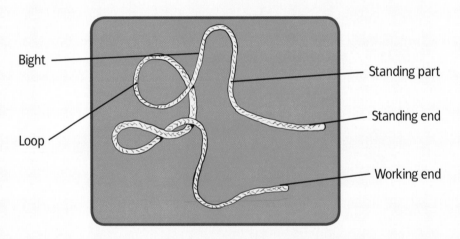

- **Working end:** the end of the rope you're using to tie a knot.
- **Standing end:** the opposite end to the working end.
- **Standing part:** any part between the two ends. It can be part of the rope already used in the knot.
- **Loop:** a loop made by turning the rope back on itself and crossing the standing part.
- **Bight:** a loop made by turning the rope back on itself without crossing the standing part.

Overhand or Thumb knot

This simple knot (which is tied in the end of a line) is quick and easy to tie, and is often used as a stopper at the end of a rope. It is the perfect first knot to learn as it forms the basis of more complicated knots.

INSTRUCTIONS:

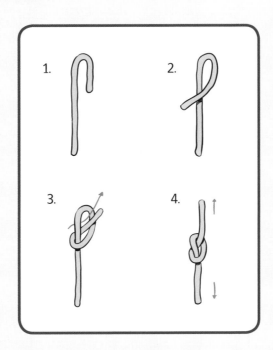

1 **Form an overhand loop,** by taking the working end in a clockwise direction over the standing end.

2 **Make a single overhand knot** by passing the working end into the loop from below. Pull through sufficient line at the working end to finish the knot.

29

The figure-of-eight knot

The figure-of-eight knot is one of the strongest stopper knots, and forms a secure and non-slip loop at the end of a rope. It is often used by mountain climbers, not only because it is so strong but also because it is easy to inspect.

A rhyme to help you remember how to tie this knot:
'Twist it once, twist it twice; pass it through and make it nice.'

INSTRUCTIONS:

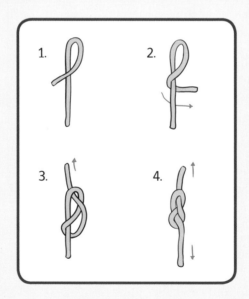

1 **Twist it once:** make an overhand loop with the working end, twisting anticlockwise.

2 **Twist it twice**: twist the loop again anticlockwise.

3 **Pass it through**: pass the working end up into the loop to complete the knot.

4 **Make it nice**: tidy up by pulling on either end of your knot.

The square or reef knot

This knot is used to tie together two working ends of the same material and size, to secure something that is not likely to move about. It lies flat when tied with cloth, making it particularly useful for bandages.

A mnemonic to help you remember how to tie this knot:
'Left over right and under, then right over left and under.'

INSTRUCTIONS:

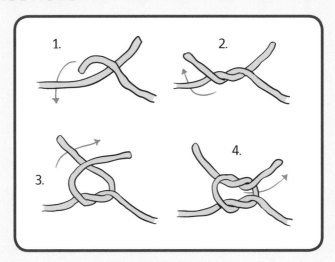

1. **Put the left-hand working end** over the right.

2. **Twist the upper working end** around, under and back to the front.

3. **Bend the working ends towards each other,** right going over left.

4. **Twist the upper working end** around, under and back to the front.

5. **Tidy up** by pulling on each working end.

The bowline

The bowline is used to make a loop at one end of a rope or line. It forms a secure loop that is easy to tie and untie, making it one of the most useful knots. It can be used for tasks such as a rope swing seat, and in the construction of a tarp shelter.

A rhyme to help you remember how to tie this knot: 'Up through the rabbit hole, round the big tree; down through the rabbit hole and off goes he.'

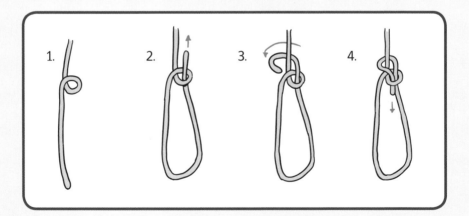

INSTRUCTIONS:

1 **Create the 'rabbit hole'** by crossing the working end over the rope to form a 'b' shape.

2 **Up through the hole:** bring the working end up through the loop you created.

3 **Round the big tree:** bring the working end around the back of the standing end.

4 **Down the rabbit hole and off he goes:** then place it back down through the loop and tighten.

MISSION ACCOMPLISHED

I verify that on this date .... I started to learn how to tie knots with my Commando Dad.

Signed: ....

CHAPTER 2:

MISSIONS IN THE GARDEN

GO ON A MINI-BEAST SAFARI

Mission brief

- **Ground:** gardens and a variety of other habitats, such as parks, woods and playing fields – wherever mini-beasts roam.
- **Situation:** any weather or season. It will affect the mini-beasts you find.
- **Mission:** to track and identify – but not capture – mini-beasts.
- **Time:** you decide the time to spend on this activity.

MISSION KEY

£ £ £ £ £   JT   AT

KIT LIST:

- A camera, if you have one, so your troopers can continue studying their small game at base camp later.

- Paper and pencil for the artistic troopers (ideally with something to lean on, such as a clipboard).

- Spotting sheet – in addition to the 'spot it' pages in this section, you can find great downloadable spotting sheets at www. wildlifewatch.org.uk/spotting-sheets.

- Binoculars if you have them, they are not strictly necessary for small game but will be popular nonetheless.

- A magnifying glass if you have one. Avoid using them directly on mini-beasts on sunny days as you will burn them.

- Insect repellent if your garden is a haven for swarms of biting insects.

- If you're away from base camp, wipes or hand sanitisers to clean hands after handling mini-beasts.

INSTRUCTIONS:

1 Make sure everyone knows that when they have permission to handle any of the mini-beasts, they must be very gentle and must place them back exactly where they found them. If you find a mini-beast that could bite or sting, explain to your troopers what it is, and why they shouldn't touch it.

2 Adopt quiet 'David Attenborough' tones and encourage the troopers to do the same. This will have no effect on the bugs whatsoever, but will avoid startling other kinds of wildlife, and will add to the anticipation.

3 Move slowly and carefully, making no sudden movements.

4 Be prepared for squeals of disgust and delight.

5 If you're anxious, don't show it. Troopers take their cues from you, and if you show you're nervous around mini-beasts they will learn to be too.

6 Challenge the misconceptions about mini-beasts. Bees aren't just stinging machines, they're arch pollinators and without them many plants and crops (including the ones we eat) would die. Flies can be a pain but they are busy workers in the garden, pollinating, helping to dispose of decaying waste and serving as a protein-rich meal for birds, frogs, spiders and other insects. Worms aren't slimy mini-snakes, they're 'nature's ploughs' turning waste into nutrient-rich soil.

7 Look for tracks. Wet mud and snow provide great opportunities to find animal tracks.

8 Take photographs and draw pictures. This will help you identify mini-beasts and their tracks later on.

NOTE

Use the mini-beast 'spot it' sheet on p.38–39 to help record what your troopers find.

Good places to look for mini-beasts in the garden include:

- In or near any kind of flowers or plants, including potted plants, window boxes, hanging baskets.
- In or near any kind of shelter, including bird boxes, the eaves of sheds and buildings, piles of wood or leaves.
- In or near any source of water, including a bird bath, pond, water butt. Don't forget your Trooper Boundary Brief – no trooper goes anywhere near water unless Commando Dad is around.
- In a shed.
- In a compost heap.
- In a hedge or bush.
- In long grass.
- Under stones and slabs. Don't forget your Trooper Boundary Brief – let them know not to go for really big stones to look under. Get Commando Dad to do any heavy lifting.
- Once 'Mission Mini-Beast' is complete, don't forget to thoroughly wash your hands.

MINI-BEAST 'SPOT IT' SHEET

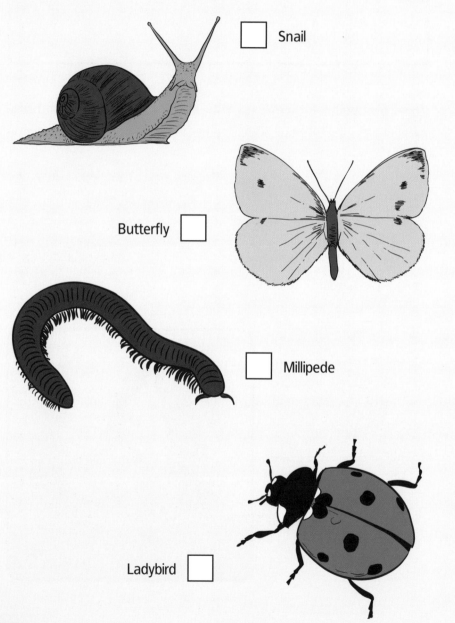

Snail ☐

Butterfly ☐

Millipede ☐

Ladybird ☐

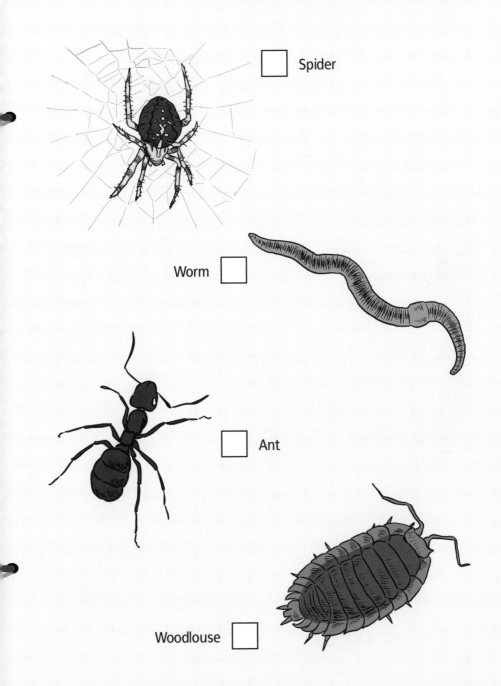

Spider ☐

Worm ☐

Ant ☐

Woodlouse ☐

Most bites and stings cause minor irritation. For more information about how to treat them, and information about what to do if a trooper has a more severe reaction, please see the NHS Choices page on Bites and Stings: www.nhs.uk/conditions/Bites-insect/Pages/Introduction.aspx.

Make your garden mini-beast friendly

 WARNING

Please ensure all ponds are covered over with safety netting if small troopers are around.

If your troopers loved looking at mini-beasts they may want to take some simple steps to attract more into the garden:

- **Provide shelter.**
  - If you have green fingers, you and your troopers can use plants that provide shelter – and food – to attract small game. Fruit trees are a favourite for mammals, birds and insects, while fragrant flowers like lavender, dandelions or bluebells will attract butterflies and bees.
  - If you don't have green fingers, a pile of wood or rocks will attract a variety of insects, such as woodlice, spiders and beetles, and require no maintenance, as will a part of your garden allowed to 'go wild' – it will soon be colonised by grasses and wild flowers.
  - A compost bin will enable you to provide shelter for worms while also reducing waste.

- **Provide food.** Find out what you want to attract to your garden, and what it feeds on. For example:

  - You can buy a variety of food for birds, but in my experience mealworm can turn any garden into a scene from the film *The Birds*.

  - Bats eats moths, which can be attracted into your garden by strong-scented flowers.

  - Do not leave milk out for hedgehogs, it makes them sick – use tap water instead.

- **Provide water.**

  - A pond, a water butt or a bowl of water are all useful sources of water.

MISSION ACCOMPLISHED

I verify that on this date .... I tracked mini-beasts with my Commando Dad.

Signed: ....

MISSION 5:
COMPLETE A GARDEN ASSAULT COURSE

Mission brief

- **Ground:** garden.
- **Situation:** dry weather and dry ground underfoot.
- **Mission:** to successfully navigate a garden assault course.
- **Time:** depends on the complexity of the course. Bear in mind it is unlikely troopers will want to do it just once, especially if they are being timed. They're likely to want to improve their score.

MISSION KEY

£ £ £ £ £ JT AT

KIT LIST:

- Obstacles for your assault course. Obviously, these will be dependent on the ability of your troopers and the space available. Here's some ideas to get you started, based on easy to obtain items that you may already have in your base camp:

  - **Ladder run:** lay out a ladder flat on the lawn (watch out for splinters if using a wooden ladder) and the troopers can bunny hop or run through it.
  - **Hula hoop:** troopers have to pick up the hula hoop, and do a couple of full spins.
  - **Skipping rope:** troopers can either complete a prescribed set of skips, or it can be placed on the ground for a tightrope walk.

- **Commando crawl**: troopers have to crawl underneath a sheet stretched out on the grass by crawling on their stomachs (just as cargo nets are used in traditional assault courses).

- **Balance beams**: a plank of wood can be used for troopers to walk across or balanced securely off the ground for older troopers. You could use bricks or breeze blocks to raise the plank a little to increase the challenge. Give it a Commando Dad Safety Check before letting the troopers across it.

- **Ball skills:**
  - Throw a ball/s into a bucket (the balls can be different sizes and the bucket further away for different abilities).
  - Kick a ball at a 'goal' you've made (doesn't have to be a traditional net – it could be an X you chalk on the wall, or a tin can you need to knock over, etc.).

- Egg and spoon challenge: troopers have to get from A to B without dropping the egg. You can make it a race if your garden is big enough. Make sure you hard boil the eggs first!

- Water trials: if the weather is hot, include water, from apple bobbing, to running through a paddling pool, to making a water slide with water and tarpaulin (with a little washing up liquid to make it slippy). Water is always a winner.

- Exercise sets: jumping jacks, sit ups and press ups all work well in a small space, and in larger spaces, you can do cartwheels and forward rolls.

- Water and a 'refs station': a designated area for troopers to get a drink.

- A finish line: even if it is just a stick lying on the ground, troopers will want something to aim for.

- A whistle to announce the race has started.

- A stopwatch: troopers are always fascinated to know how long they have taken and may want to do it again straight away to improve their time.

Older troopers can help you design and lay out the course. They'll also be able to do a dummy run so that you can make sure it's tried and tested.

INSTRUCTIONS:

1 **Plan your course.** Include what you have in your garden – including trees, rope swings, low walls, etc. – and any play equipment (trampoline, etc.).

2 **Try to mix up different skills.** A variety of balance, agility and speed tests, etc. keeps things interesting and gives everyone the opportunity to be good at something.

3 Give your garden a **Commando Dad Safety Check for unintended obstacles,** such as holes and sharp edges, which may cause injuries when tackled at high speed.

4 **Set up your course and drinks station.**

5 **Make the first obstacle the easiest.**

6 **Explain the rules.** Make sure troopers know what's expected, ideally demonstrating each one yourself – or by an older trooper.

7 **Give the race a 'proper' start,** either by a countdown and blowing a whistle, or by shouting, 'Ready, steady, go!'

8 **Where you can join in, do,** but make sure you're keeping an eye on proceedings.

9 **If you've said you'll record times, do.** Make sure you, or someone else, are on hand to record times as troopers will want to know their times to the nanosecond.

10 **Be supportive.** Make sure you shout encouragement and clap, and get the early finishers to do the same (as well as any other spectators).

11 **Tidy up.** When the game is over, get the troops to help you tidy everything away.

MISSION ACCOMPLISHED

I verify that on this date .... I completed a tricky assault course with my Commando Dad.

Signed: ....

PLAY DODGE SPONGE

Mission brief

- **Ground:** garden, or any open space.
- **Situation:** warm sunny days. Be aware this game is noisy.
- **Mission:** to get all of the opposing team out by hitting them with wet sponges, while ensuring you dodge the ones they throw at you.
- **Time:** the game can be over in a matter of minutes if your troopers aim straight and true, but expect to play multiple games.

MISSION KEY

£ £ £ £ £   JT   AT

KIT LIST:

- Buckets.
- Water.
- One sponge per player, if possible.
- Lightweight sports clothes (such as shorts/leggings and a T-shirt) or swimwear for troopers as everyone is going to get very wet. If inviting troopers from other units over, make sure they know they'll need to bring this kit and a spare set of clothes.

- Game markings (anything will do to demark these areas – even a broom laid out):
  - A centre line.
  - A 'prison section' if you have more than two players taking part. This is a place where players who are 'out' must go (*see diagram*).
- Towels.
- Waterproof sunscreen: reapply regularly on really sunny days.

To reduce water usage, you could use water you've previously captured in a water butt, or water that's been in a paddling pool.

INSTRUCTIONS:

1 **Lay out your pitch:** a centre line and a prison section for each team.

Team B's Prison	Team A	Team B	Team A's Prison

2 **Place water buckets on the centre line** but to the side so they don't get kicked over. This will ensure the troops can get to them easily if they need to wet their sponge, but they won't accidentally back into them.

3 **Make rules and make sure everyone knows them.** I have put my dodge sponge rules below, but feel free to make up your own depending on your troopers' ages and ability. Don't be afraid to change rules on the fly.

4 **Divide the troops into teams.** Try to make them as equally matched as possible. I find that eight is usually the maximum for this game, especially as you will need to keep an eye on proceedings.

5 **If you can join in, do.** Everyone loves hitting a Commando Dad with a sponge.

6 **Ensure every trooper has a sponge if possible.**

7 **Give it a 'proper' start**, either by a countdown and blowing a whistle, or by shouting, 'Ready, steady, go!'

8 **Tidy up.** When the game is over, get the troops to help you tidy everything away. If your troopers get muddy and you have a garden hose, hose them down at the end of the game. My troopers loved it when I shouted, 'Arms in the air like you just don't care!' before giving them a good soaking.

DODGE SPONGE RULES

- Always aim below the head. Troopers deliberately ignoring this rule will be out of the game.
- If you hear the whistle, you must stop play.
- If you are hit by a sponge, you are out and have to stand at the 'prison section'.
- If a player catches a sponge while in play, a teammate in their prison section can come back into the game.
- You can only hold a sponge for 10 seconds (and you may have to dip it in the bucket during that time), otherwise you forfeit, or lose, your turn and must pass it (not throw it) to the opposing team.

- If there are only two players left, I like to go to a duel situation. You flip a coin to see who goes first, the two opponents stand back to back at the centre line with a sponge, they walk ten paces away from each other, turn and 'shoot'...

MISSION ACCOMPLISHED

I verify that on this date .... I played a fierce game of dodge sponge with my Commando Dad.

Signed: ....

MISSION 7:
PLAY BOMB BURST

Mission brief

- **Ground:** garden, or any open space.
- **Situation:** warm sunny days. Be aware this game is noisy.
- **Mission:** to catch a water bomb as many times as possible before it bursts.
- **Time:** depends upon the skill of your troopers and the number of water bombs at your disposal.

MISSION KEY

£ £ £ £ £   JT   AT

KIT LIST:

- Water balloons. You can buy small balloons from a good toyshop.
- Water.
- An ammo store. Somewhere to keep your bombs until you need them – a bucket or washing-up bowl are good options.
- A watch, if timing.

INSTRUCTIONS:

1. **Prepare your water bombs.** If you have an older trooper in your unit, they can help you do this, and use an outdoor tap if you have one. Simply stretch the balloon opening over the tap, and <u>slowly</u> turn on the water to fill up your water bomb, and tie up the end using a thumb knot (*see 'Mission 3: Knots' in Adventures in Base Camp*) Don't overfill as this makes it difficult to tie up your balloon and means your water bomb may suffer premature detonation.

2. **Put the bombs in the ammo store.** Make sure it is part-filled with water as this will relieve pressure and prevent your water bombs bursting.

3. **Make sure players know the only rule.** Water bombs must be thrown gently <u>to</u> another player, not at them.

4. **Divide players into pairs.** You can either:

   - Have them facing each other. Each player must take a step back and throw back and forth once. If the bomb survives they must take and another step back and throw back and forth again, etc.

   - Have them standing a set distance apart and throw back and forth from that position.

5. **Give your troopers a demonstration** of a good way to throw (underarm) and catch (*see overleaf*) a water bomb to make it last as long as possible.

6. If you can join in, do.

7. **You can time how long a bomb stays in play before bursting.** Or get troopers to count along out loud every time it is caught.

   If playing in teams, the winning team is the one with an intact water bomb. If a single pair is playing, the loser is the one that bursts the last water bomb.

8 **Tidy up.** When the game is over, get the troops to help you tidy everything away.

Make sure you don't overfill the water bombs, fill them with warm water or leave them in the sun. These will all increase the risk of them bursting.

How to catch a water bomb

In order to minimise the chance of popping a water bomb, you must minimise the force of impact.

- Use both hands.
- Don't let it come to a dead stop in your hands. Instead, catch it but keep your arms moving, if possible in the same trajectory the balloon was on.
- Bring hands to a slow stop.

Other games with water bombs

There are a variety of games you can play with water bombs:

- Water bomb and ladle race. Could be a twist to up the ante on your Garden Assault Course.
- Target practice. Each player wears a cycle helmet with a colander attached to the top. Most helmets have ventilation slots in them, so pass either string or small cable ties through the colander holes and helmet slots, and fasten as tightly as possible. The aim is to get as many intact water bombs into your colander as possible, without any bursting all over your head.

- Throw in the towel. One team (of two players) uses a large towel to throw a water bomb to the other team who must catch it in a towel without it bursting.

- If there are any intact bombs left at the end of proceedings, you might want to consider calling a suspension to the regular rules, and bring into play the 'Free-For-All Rule' – that is, all other rules are suspended, and everyone grabs a water bomb, acquires a target and gives them a soaking!

MISSION ACCOMPLISHED

I verify that on this date .... I caught, and threw, water bombs with my Commando Dad.

Signed: ....

NAVIGATE BY THE STARS

Mission brief

- **Ground:** garden, open field or a large park.
- **Situation:** a clear night, in a location with as little light pollution as possible.
- **Mission:** to use the stars to find where north is or, to be precise, Polaris (the North Star).
- **Time:** 30 minutes.

MISSION KEY

£££££ JT AT

KIT LIST:

- Torch, to illuminate your path when walking in open spaces.
- Notepad and pen/pencil to draw the constellations you see.

INSTRUCTIONS:

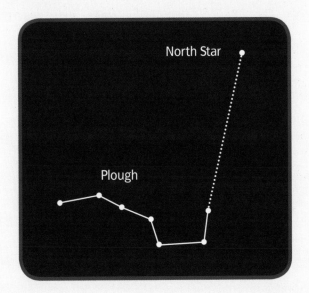

1. **Find the Plough.** This constellation is made of seven stars and as long as you have a clear night, should be quite easy to identify.

2. **Locate the last two stars that make up the blade section.** Then, follow them upwards in a straight line, four times the distance between those two stars. There you will find Polaris, or the North Star.
   This star sits directly over the North Pole.

3. **Head towards it**, and you will be marching north.

Another way of finding north

There's another constellation – Cassiopeia – that can also help find the North Star. Cassiopeia and the Plough sit opposite each other, and circle each other around the North Star. Therefore, if the Plough is low or obscured, Cassiopeia will be high in the sky.

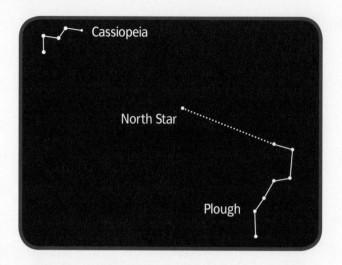

NOTE

If your trooper enjoyed star spotting, there are a few other constellations that are easy to spot. The plough actually forms part of the constellation Ursa Major (Latin for Great Bear). Polaris is actually at the end of the tail of Ursa Minor (or Little Bear). In the South you'll see Orion's Belt and the brightest star in the night sky, Sirius.

For useful resources on how to identify major constellations, go to the Mission Adventure section on www.commandodad.com.

MISSION ACCOMPLISHED

I verify that on this date .... I found Polaris and started to learn how to navigate at night with my Commando Dad.

Signed: ....

CHAPTER 3:

MISSIONS IN THE COOKHOUSE

MISSION 9:
MAKE GLOOP

Mission brief

- **Ground:** cookhouse or outside, if warm enough.
- **Situation:** an activity for Commando Dads and troopers that love getting messy.
- **Mission:** to create a non-Newtonian fluid, which is a substance that is both a liquid and a solid.
- **Time:** about 10 minutes to make, but will entertain for much longer.

MISSION KEY

£££££   JT AT

KIT LIST:

- 450 g cornflour.
- 475 ml water.
- Something for each trooper to make their gloop in: an adequately sized mixing bowl, a tub, a plastic tray, etc.
- Food colouring, if you want a coloured gloop.
- Eye dropper, to dispense food colouring.
- It is inevitable that there's going to be mess but gloop is straightforward to clean up afterwards. Nevertheless, you may wish to employ the following:

  - Aprons/your old T-shirts turned inside out, etc. to protect clothes.

  - Newspaper on the floor (although it can easily be mopped up).

- Music speaker and cling film if you want to make the gloop 'dance'.

INSTRUCTIONS:

Your trooper can:

1 **Add the cornflour to the bowl** or whatever they're making their gloop in. It's best to use a spoon, not because the measurement has to be exact but because if it's tipped too quickly you'll get a cloud of dust that sticks to everything and gets everywhere, and much coughing will ensue.

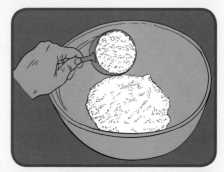

2 **Add the water.** Add just a little at a time until you get the right consistency, which is best described as soft and silky honey.

3 **Mix.** I advocate troopers use their hands rather than a spoon because the slower they stir the stiffer the gloop becomes, making it even harder to stir… It's a viscous cycle.

4 **Add colour.** A few drops of colour into the gloop are usually enough. Mix with hands. Troopers usually love to get their hands in gloop, but if they're not too keen, or you're worried about staining, use plastic gloves.

⑤ Tidy up. When the troops have tired of gloop, it's time to tidy up. The gloop should be put in a plastic bag which can be fastened. You can keep it for playing another time, or dispose of it in the bin. As the cornflour and water won't stay mixed indefinitely, <u>do not</u> put it down the sink as it could clog the pipes. Small amounts can be wiped off most surfaces easily. If any has gone on the floor, it's time to get the mop out. You won't have a problem getting a trooper to take on this task.

Here are some fun things you can do with gloop:

- You and the troopers can roll it into a ball between your hands. When you stop the movement and simply hold the gloop in your hands, it will turn to liquid and run through your fingers.

- Try slapping it or punching it and removing your hand quickly. It won't splash but instead harden around the impact. Non-Newtonian fluids are used in body armour and this illustrates why they're so effective.

- Imitate quicksand.
  - Immerse your hand completely and try to move it around quickly. The more you try the harder it becomes. Then try to grab the gloop and pull your hand out.
  - Drop in a moulded plastic toy, and then try to rescue it from the quicksand.

- Throw it against something solid, if outside. It will be a fluid as it travels through the air but become hard on impact.

- If you want to make the gloop dance, take a speaker cone, line it with cling film and spoon some of the gloop onto it. Then play music and watch how it forms strange tendrils that seem to dance.

It is possible to make glow-in-the-dark gloop by substituting normal water for tonic water. You'll need a black or ultra-violet light to be able to really see its luminescence.

 ## THE SCIENCE BIT

Cornflour is made of long, stringy polymers. When water is applied they spread out. When you touch the fluid slowly, these polymers glide past each other easily. However, if pressure is applied, or you move the mixture too quickly, the polymers join together and the mixture feels solid.

The beauty of gloop is its unusual properties. As long as pressure is being applied it acts as a solid. When there is no pressure it acts as a liquid. Liquids that don't act as 'everyday' liquids such as gloop are classed as non-Newtonian fluids.

MISSION ACCOMPLISHED

I verify that on this date .... I defied the laws of science with my Commando Dad.

Signed: ....

MISSION 10:
MAKE MODELLING DOUGH

Mission brief

- **Ground:** cookhouse or outside, if warm enough.
- **Situation:** when creativity strikes.
- **Mission:** to make clay for modelling. Older troopers may want to use it in the next mission, 'Indoor Volcano'.
- **Time:** takes about an hour to make, which includes cooling time for the dough.

MISSION KEY

£ £ £ £ £   JT   AT

KIT LIST:

- 300 g plain flour.
- 100 g salt.
- 360 ml boiling water.
- 30 g cream of tartar.
- A few drops of food colouring (if you want coloured dough).
- Large mixing bowl.
- Wooden spoon.
- Eye dropper, to dispense food colouring.
- 2 tablespoons of cooking oil (any type).
- If using colour and you're concerned about staining:
  - Plastic gloves for troopers' hands.
  - Aprons/your old T-shirts turned inside out, etc. to protect clothes.
  - Plastic trays/plastic placemats/cling film to protect light or wooden work surfaces.
- Airtight plastic tub or bag to keep it in between plays.

WARNING

These instructions include Commando Dad using boiling water, so don't forget your Trooper Boundary Brief. Please exercise special caution when using hot water around your troopers as it can scald and burn.

INSTRUCTIONS:

1 **Mix the dry ingredients in the bowl:** the flour, salt and cream of tartar.

2 **Add the oil.** If you only want one colour, you can add the food colouring now. If you intend to make multiple colours, you can knead the colours in later.

3 **Add the boiling water.** Use your common sense here and be careful with troopers around.

4 **Mix with a wooden spoon** until all of the ingredients are combined and then leave to cool.

If you've added a single colour, or are happy to have no colour at all, then play can commence.

If you're making different colours, you will knead them in (*see below*).

How to knead in colour:

- **Prepare the surface** by sprinkling flour on a flat, clean surface.

- **Make sure troopers wash and dry their hands, then put flour on them.** It may be a sticky job, but someone's got to do it. If troopers are using gloves, they can put them on after they've dried their hands.

- **Trooping the colour.**

Get the troopers to:

- Separate the dough into balls, depending on how many different colours you're making.

- Push their finger into each ball, about halfway.

- Add <u>two drops</u> of colour in the hole (they can always add more).

- Knead the colour through, by pressing, folding, rolling and stretching the dough with their hands.

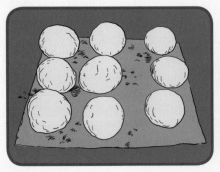 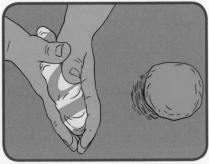

5 **Tidy up.** When the game is over, get the troops to help you wash up and tidy everything away. Your modelling dough should be stored in an airtight plastic bag or tub between uses to prevent it drying out. If it does get left out, you can reanimate it by adding water (a teaspoon at a time) and working it through the mixture.

The opportunities are endless for modelling, but my troops always liked bold, colourful and easily recognisable shapes:

- Figures, such as starfish and flowers, are good choices.
- It's good if everyone attempts to make a model of the same thing, as troopers will enjoy critiquing your work. They can be ferociously honest critics, so 'stand by'.

It is also possible to add essences to your modelling dough – vanilla smells particularly good – but I abandoned this idea as it makes it smell so nice that troopers want to eat it. This recipe is too salty for that to be a good idea.

MISSION ACCOMPLISHED

I verify that on this date .... I unleashed my creativity by making modelling dough with my Commando Dad.

Signed: ....

MISSION 11:
MAKE AN INDOOR VOLCANO

Mission brief

- **Ground:** cookhouse or outside, if warm enough.
- **Situation:** is that a rumble coming from the family volcano?
- **Mission:** to create our very own trooper volcano.
- **Time:** 30 minutes minimum to make the volcano.

MISSION KEY

£££££ JT AT

KIT LIST:

- 10 g baking soda.
- A squirt of washing up liquid.
- Orange or red food colouring.
- Warm water.
- Vinegar.
- A small plastic bottle.
- Eye dropper, to dispense food colouring.
- Card or paper that has to be taller than the bottle when in a cone shape.

- Sticky tape.
- Modelling clay (or you can use the modelling dough you made in the last activity).
- Something for your volcano to be placed in that can catch the lava but not hide the action, such as a baking tray, plastic tray, etc.
- Aprons/your old T-shirts turned inside out, etc. to protect clothes.

INSTRUCTIONS:

1 **Make a mountain:** Take the paper or card (the smaller it is the fewer ingredients you are going to need to use) and make a cone shape around your small plastic bottle; the neck of the bottle will be fully hidden with whatever material you choose to cover your cone. This is the basic shape of your mountain. Use sticky tape to secure it into a cone shape and attach it to the plastic bottle at the neck. Cover the cone with modelling clay or dough and you can get creative here, working together with the troops to make the mountain as realistic as possible. Make sure you fully hide the neck of the bottle.

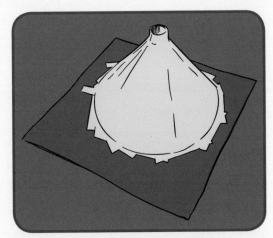

2 **Fill most of the bottle with warm water.** Warm water is better than cold and creates a better eruption because the heat increases the chemical reaction.

3 Add a few drops of food colouring.

4 Add a short squirt of washing up liquid. This will help to trap the bubbles produced by the reaction, resulting in a better lava flow.

5 Add 2 teaspoons of baking soda. The volcano is now prepped but can't erupt without the vinegar.

6 Eruption! Add the vinegar slowly – too quickly and you'll get the same explosive reaction as a can of fizzy drink that's opened after being shaken vigorously.

7 Recharge. You can recharge your volcano by adding more baking soda and vinegar.

8 Tidy up. When the fun is over, make sure the troops help you clear the mess away. Liquids can be tipped safely down the sink.

 ## THE SCIENCE BIT

The eruption is caused by the mixing of two chemicals: weak acetic acid (vinegar) and sodium bicarbonate (baking soda). Together, they create carbon dioxide gas, which is also in volcanoes. The reaction causes pressure to build up inside the bottle, until the gas bubbles escape from the bottle.

MISSION ACCOMPLISHED

I verify that on this date .... I enjoyed an explosive time with my Commando Dad.

Signed: ....

MISSION 12:
MAKE INDOOR RAIN

Mission brief

- **Ground:** cookhouse.
- **Situation:** a perfect rainy day activity – you can explain the weather!
- **Mission:** to capture Britain's most popular weather in a jar.
- **Time:** once you have everything to hand, about 5 minutes.

MISSION KEY

£ £ £ £ £   JT AT

KIT LIST:

- Hot water (just off the boil).
- A large clear glass jar, tall vase, tall glass or tall measuring jug.
- A tray of ice cubes.
- A bowl.

INSTRUCTIONS:

1 **Create your rain catcher.** Pour a small amount of hot water into your jar (or vase). Fill it to no more than a third.

2 **Capture the heat.** Place the bowl upright on top, and make sure there are no gaps so the heat is trapped inside the jar. Leave it for a few minutes until the jar is misting up.

3 **Introduce cold air.** Add ice cubes to the bowl.

4 **Looks like rain again.** Water droplets will start to collect on the side of the jar, and will drop down back into the water, just like rain.

 THE SCIENCE BIT

The hot, moist air in the jar rises and hits the bottom of the cold bowl. The water vapour then condenses into water droplets on the bottom of the bowl.

When they become heavy enough to fall, they drop like rain. This is what happens in the atmosphere to cause rain.

- **Evaporation.** The sun shines on the water on earth: rivers, lakes, seas, etc. and turns the water to vapour.
- **Condensation.** The warm moist air rises from earth, and meets cold air high in the atmosphere and condenses into water droplets. We see this condensed water vapour as clouds.
- **Precipitation.** When the water becomes heavy enough to fall, we get rain – or hail, sleet or snow.
  - **Snow crystals** are formed when water droplets in clouds become very cold. They fall from the cloud, forming snowflakes. To make it all the way to the ground, the air must be freezing. If not, the snowflakes melt and turn to rain.
  - **Sleet** is a mixture of snow and rain.
  - **Hail** is hard frozen rain.
- **Run-off.** The water from the rain is restored to the rivers, lakes, seas, etc.

If you're doing this mission on a rainy day, get the troops suited and booted and get out in it. Go and jump in some puddles, and then ask the troops what they think happens to the puddles when the sun comes out. They don't disappear: they change from one form (a liquid: water) to another (a gas: water vapour).

MISSION ACCOMPLISHED

I verify that on this date .... I harnessed the weather together with my Commando Dad.

Signed: ....

MISSION 13:
MAKE INVISIBLE INK

Mission brief

- **Ground:** depending on your writing medium, anywhere in base camp.
- **Situation:** not weather dependent.
- **Mission:** to create invisible messages, and reveal how to make them visible again.
- **Time:** the ink can take up to 30 minutes to dry.

MISSION KEY

£ £ £ £ £   JT   AT

KIT LIST:

- White paper.
- Writing implement: cotton bud, a paintbrush, cocktail stick, etc.
- Then choose the rest of your kit list from the options below:

For heat-activated invisible ink

- Ink: this can be made from a variety of liquids:
  - Acidic juice such as lemon, plus a couple of teaspoons of water.
  - Vinegar.

- White wine.
- Milk.

- A heat source: choose the one most appropriate for your trooper's ability and your own comfort level – and supervise at all times:
  - A light bulb.
  - An iron.
  - A hairdryer.
  - A radiator (not the best choice if your troops are impatient).

For glow-in-the-dark invisible ink

- Ink:
  - Tonic water.
  - Vaseline.
- An ultraviolet light source to reveal the messages.

Wax crayon invisible ink

- White wax crayon.
- Paint.
- A paintbrush.

WARNING

These instructions include using heat sources, such as a hot iron. Please exercise caution, common sense and close supervision if you intend to let your trooper undertake these tasks themselves. A Trooper Boundary Brief is essential for this mission.

INSTRUCTIONS:

To create a hidden message:

1. Take your paper and whichever ink you're using, and write your message. Make the messages clear and, ideally, short.

2. Let the paper dry (this is not necessary if you used the wax crayon method). When the paper is completely dry, you may want to write a message over the top – a decoy message – in order to make it harder to find. Use pencil or ballpoint pens, as felt tips or fountain pens could run into your invisible ink.

To reveal a hidden message:

1. In the case of **heat-activated invisible ink**, the paper needs to be gently heated until the message is revealed. This can be achieved by either using a hairdryer or making use of the base camp iron (Commando Dad to take on this important task).

2. For **glow-in-the-dark invisible ink**, simply shine an ultraviolet light on the paper to reveal the message.

3. For **wax crayon invisible ink**, you can paint over the page to reveal the message, or if you have no paints, use colouring pencils or felt tips.

This is a great activity for using in other games that require clues such as Target Acquisition.

 NOTE

The phrase 'read between the lines' is thought to have originated from the practice of writing messages in disappearing ink and hiding them between lines of visible text.

MISSION ACCOMPLISHED

I verify that on this date .... I channelled my inner spy with my Commando Dad.

Signed: ....

MISSION 14:
MAKE A LAVA LAMP

Mission brief
- **Ground:** cookhouse.
- **Situation:** not weather dependent.
- **Mission:** to create a chemical reaction that will send coloured bubbles through your lava lamp.
- **Time:** about 30 minutes.

MISSION KEY

£ £ £ £ £   JT AT

KIT LIST:

- A clean, clear plastic bottle with a cap (to prevent oily spillages) or large jar with lid.
- Water.
- Vegetable oil. You can use cooking oil that you've used, just make sure you sieve it.

- Food colouring.
- Eye dropper, to dispense food colouring.
- An effervescent tablet, such as those used for heartburn and indigestion.

INSTRUCTIONS:

1 **Pour water in the bottle** until it is about a third full.

2 **Add the vegetable oil** until it nearly fills the bottle. You'll need to leave a gap at the top.

3 **Add colour.** Put about 10 drops of food colouring into the bottle. Put the cap on and wait for the colour to drop through the oil and mix with the water at the bottom of the bottle.

4 **Crush up the effervescent tablet** using two spoons, while waiting for the colour to settle.

5 **Open the bottle and pour in the crushed tablet.** The minute the crushed pieces hit the water, it will start to produce bubbles.

6 **Tidy up.** If you want to use the lava lamp later, simply screw on the cap. You'll just need to add more effervescent tablets later to start the chemical reaction again. If you have finished and wish to dispose of the lamp, put it in the bin. Do not tip it down the sink as it will cause problems as it solidifies.

THE SCIENCE BIT

Oil and water don't mix and so they remain separate in the bottle. The water is at the bottom of the bottle because it has a higher density than the oil. The effervescent tablet releases small bubbles of carbon dioxide gas that rise to the top because they are less dense than the water and oil around them. The gas takes the coloured water with it and when it escapes at the top, the coloured water falls all the way back through the oil to rest at the bottom again.

MISSION ACCOMPLISHED

I verify that on this date .... I created an ingenious lava lamp with my Commando Dad.

Signed: ....

MISSION 15:
PEEL, GRATE AND CUT FRUIT AND VEGETABLES

Mission brief

- **Ground:** cookhouse.
- **Situation:** mealtimes. You may be surprised how keen your troopers are to help you cook.
- **Mission:** to equip your trooper with the skills they need to help you in the cookhouse.
- **Time:** give yourself plenty of time to prepare food, as you don't want the added pressure of having to hurry.

MISSION KEY

£££££   JT   AT

KIT LIST:

- Peeler.
- Grater.
- Small kitchen knife.
- Chopping board.

- Something safe for the troops to stand on so the counter is at about waist height. It's best to use a step stool that is made for the task of raising your troopers up to the correct height.
- Suitable foodstuffs.

INSTRUCTIONS:

You will need to use your own common sense and judgement to decide which of these tasks your trooper is ready to take on. If you feel that your trooper is not ready for any of these skills, you can still get them involved in the kitchen: teach them to sieve, wash vegetables, measure out ingredients, whisk or stir, and crack eggs into a bowl, for example.

For all of these tasks, your close supervision is key, and give a Trooper Boundary Brief.

Peeling

A great food to start peeling is carrots. They are easy to peel, allowing the troops to build up their peeling skills.

Your trooper will need to:

1 **Wash and dry hands.**

2 **Wash carrots** if they're dirty.

3 **Hold the carrot at the top end,** and rest the other end on the clean chopping board.

4 Take the peeler and, starting halfway down the carrot, **run the peeler along the length of the carrot away from themselves**. If they're nervous to begin with, they may press hard and take quite a lot of carrot when they remove the peel. Just reassure them that they don't need to press so hard.

5 **Twist the carrot** so that the whole bottom half gets peeled.

6 **Turn the carrot** around and hold it at the peeled, bottom end, and repeat the process to peel the top half of the carrot.

7 When the carrot is peeled, **the top and bottom need to be cut off**. If you're confident for your trooper to take this on, follow the instructions below. If not, you can do this task.

8 **Wash and dry hands.**

9 **Tidy up.** When all peeling has been completed, the peelings need to be removed and either put in the bin or into your compost bin.

   If you're not using the carrots for dinner, let your troopers eat them as a snack.

Grating

The key point to teach your trooper about grating is that you do not have to grate every bit of the food. They'll need to have some food left to protect their fingers. A great food for learning grating skills is cheese. It's nice and soft, and hands won't get wet and slippery, like they may with other foodstuffs, such as carrots and apples.

   Your trooper will need to:

1 **Wash and dry hands.**

2 **Unwrap the cheese** (you may want to cut the cheese down to a manageable size).

3 Place the grater on the clean chopping board and **hold it firmly by the handle**.

4 **Hold the cheese at the top of the grater and rub it against the grater in an up-and-down motion.**

5 **Repeat** the process until there is enough cheese grated, or there is only a small piece of cheese left.

6 **Tap the grater** to dislodge all of the cheese that might be caught in the blades.

Take the cheese off the chopping board and, if it's not being used straight away, put it in a bowl or tub, cover it and put it in the fridge.

7 **Wash and dry hands.**

8 **Tidy up** and put everything away.

A Commando Dad leads by example. Always make sure that you demonstrate the safe knife skills in the cookhouse that you want your troopers to follow.

Cutting

i **KNIFE TIPS**

You can buy knives specifically for troopers to use in the cookhouse, or use a smaller adult one.

The knives should be sharp, as blunt knives won't cut through easily and this may encourage the troopers to press on the knife and try to use force to cut. This may cause the blade to bounce or slide off the food and onto unsuspecting fingers.

There are two safe methods of cutting for your trooper to learn, both of which keep their fingers away from the knife blade.

- The bridge (good for cutting food into segments).
- The claw (good for slicing).

If you'd like your troopers to practise these skills before they pick up a knife, they can use the modelling dough they made and a plastic knife.

The bridge

Good foods to practise this technique on are big strawberries and normal-sized tomatoes (not cherry tomatoes which may put little fingers too near the knife for beginners). They are the right size to hold and let the trooper focus all their concentration on their knife skills.

Your trooper will need to:

1 **Wash and dry hands**.

2 **Remove the stalk,** if the fruit has one, and put the fruit on the clean chopping board.

3 Make a bridge over the tomato with their hand, by **putting their fingers on one side and their thumb on the other**. The space between their hand and the tomato will look like a bridge. Make sure the space between your trooper's palm and the tomato is sufficient to cut safely.

4 Take the knife in their other hand and **make sure that the blade is facing downwards**.

5 Guide the knife under the bridge and **use that forward motion to cut** the tomato down the middle.

6 **Keeping the knife in the tomato, draw the knife part way out of the bridge** (but not all the way).

7 **Repeat.**

8 When the tomato has been cut in half, put down the knife.

9 Place the tomato half flat side down and cut it in exactly the same way.

10 Repeat until the tomato is in four segments.

11 When all chopping is complete, **wash and dry hands**.

12 **Tidy up** and put everything away.

The claw

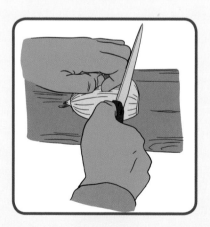

This method will protect fingers and is a key knife skill to take into adulthood. If I have to hold the food I'm cutting, I use the claw technique. A good food to practise this technique on is celery, and the ridges make it easier for your trooper to grip it.

Your trooper will need to:

1 **Wash and dry hands.**

2 **Wash your vegetable** if it is dirty (you might want to take the top and bottom of the vegetable off for your trooper) and put it on the clean chopping board.

3 **Make a claw with the non-cutting hand,** by keeping their fingers close together and partially curling their fingers inwards (this will keep their fingers away from the knife). They must keep the ends of their fingers vertical though. Thumbs must be kept hidden.

4 **Put their claw on the vegetable near where you are going to make the cut.** Adjust the fingers so that the claw shape remains intact and is holding the vegetable steady.

5 Pick up the knife and **ensure the blade is pointing downwards.**

6 **Slice through the vegetable carefully,** using the claw as a guide.

7 **Move their fingers back** and slice through the vegetable again.

8 **Repeat** until you have enough slices.

9 When all slicing is complete, **wash and dry hands.**

10 **Tidy up** and put everything away.

GOLDEN RULES FOR USING A KNIFE

- Never hold the food you're cutting in your hand. It should always be cut on a chopping board.
- Always hold the knife carefully.
- Always cut away from you.
- If your hand is wet and feels slippery, stop and dry your hands.
- Never move around the kitchen with a knife in your hand.
- Never drop a sharp knife into the washing up bowl, always leave it at the side of the sink where it can be seen and washed carefully.

MISSION ACCOMPLISHED

I verify that on this date .... I first started to learn valuable cookhouse skills with my Commando Dad.

Signed: ....

SECTION 2:

ADVENTURES IN TRANSIT

MISSION 16:
ENGAGE IN SOME GAMES IN TRANSIT

When engaging in mid-term deployments of your troops – be it to school, on holiday, or to the local shops – it always pays to have an engaging activity in your armoury.

There are three fail-safe activities that require no special equipment:

- Spotting games.
- Chasing games.
- Leading games.

All the activities in the Adventures in Transit section have the same mission key. They are designed to include everyone.

THE GOLDEN RULES OF ADVENTURES IN TRANSIT

They need to:

- Engage everyone in the unit and require no particular skill (so everyone is on an equal footing).
- Be simple to understand and play.
- Require no special equipment (you are in transit and it's just one more thing to remember).
- Be able to be played for a long time, if need be.
- Not annoy others, if travelling on public transport.
- Not distract the driver, if the unit is in a car.

INSTRUCTIONS:
SPOTTING GAMES

Best for: quickly engaging all the troops in a common goal during mid-term deployments.

- **I Spy**: The original and still the best. 'I spy with my little eye, something beginning with…' and the rest of the players have to find something beginning with that letter. After every player has had a go, you can ask for clues.

- **Mini Cheddar**: 5 points for a yellow car, 10 points for a Mini and 25 points for a yellow Mini (the elusive Mini Cheddar). The golden rule is that you only allow one 'unconfirmed' sighting per trooper in every game, or your trooper will be 'finding' yellow Minis down every side street. The first one to 100 points wins.

- **Car Pool**: Everyone playing picks a car colour. Taking it in turns, they then have to spot seven cars of that colour followed by a black car to win a frame. If another player sees a white car, then they have the cue ball and the game reverts to them. For younger troopers you can reduce the number of coloured cars.

- **The Rainbow Game**: A game where you spot colours on any object – including animals, plants and people. You start with red, and when that colour has been exhausted you can switch to yellow, pink, green, purple, orange, blue, etc.

CHASING GAMES

Best for: yomping cross wide open spaces. A running game has the power to energise them while walking to a destination. Just remember to keep the game moving in the right direction (that is, towards your end point).

- **The Hulk**: As a child of the 1970s, I cannot resist this game. When out walking from A to B just stop suddenly and say in a deadpan voice: 'Don't make me angry. You wouldn't like me when I'm angry.' You then tell the players the point of safety they must race towards as you transform. Roaring as you chase them is a necessity.

- **Greyhounds**: You are the rabbit and the greyhounds (the other players) give chase. The winner is the trooper that catches you. They then become the rabbit. Even better if you can add a running commentary throughout 'and the trooper at the rear is closing in on the pack…', etc.

- **Tag**: A group of players (two or more) decide who is going to be 'it'. 'It' then chases the others to get close enough to 'tag' them with a touch of their hand. The 'tagged' player is now 'it'. The game resumes with the new 'it' chasing the others.

- **Bear Hunt**: A variation on Tag. The first 'it' is a bear and the other players must choose an animal to be, for the bear to hunt. It doesn't have to be an animal that lives in the same habitat; I've played it with chicken and tortoises, for example. The bear announces the animal they're going to hunt and chases after that player. When the bear is closing in, the chosen prey can shout the name of another animal in the game and the bear must chase after them. If the bear does catch their prey, then that animal becomes the hunter.

LEADING GAMES

Best for: leading the whole unit to victory during light-order missions.

- **Sound Off**: An effective way to keep everyone moving in the same direction. Everyone falls in behind the leader who leads the singing, and as the music marks the cadence of the marching, you'll need an uptempo tune (think of the US Army marching songs). Try to make the lyrics funny as that will take their mind off the walking. For example:

  - Leader: I don't know but I've been told.

  - *(Followers repeat: I don't know but I've been told.)*

  - Leader: Your smelly daddy is really old.

  - *(Followers repeat.)*

  - Leader: I don't know but it's been said.

  - *(Followers repeat.)*

  - Leader: Your mum's got no hair on her head.

  - *(Followers repeat.)*

- **Follow My Leader**: Everyone falls in behind the leader, who sets the marching style. The only rule is they must keep moving towards your destination, and so marches can be as inventive as their imagination allows. Swap out the leader if you can see they're flagging. Best for when you are not too pressed for time as the leader sets the pace and younger troopers will naturally be slower.

- **Leader of the Pack**: A fast-paced game for older troopers. The pack marches in single file and when you say 'All Change!' the player at the back of the line jogs to the front and becomes the leader. They have to introduce something for the pack to do (clap, for example). When everyone is clapping, again, you call out, 'All Change!' The new leader introduces a different activity for the troopers to do (lifting both hands above the head, for example).

When travelling with troops in crowded areas or at night, make sure you 'number off'. Every member of the unit is assigned a number, with you at 'One'. When you say 'Number Off: One' then all the troops repeat their number 'Two', 'Three', 'Four', etc. This is a really effective and quick way of making sure the unit is together.

MISSION ACCOMPLISHED

I verify that on this date .... I had adventures while on the move with my Commando Dad.

Signed: ....

SECTION 3:

ADVENTURES IN THE GREAT OUTDOORS

CHAPTER 4:
MISSIONS IN THE WOODS

MISSION 17:
CLIMB A TREE

Mission brief
- **Ground:** the woods.
- **Situation:** you are faced with a tree that's calling out to be climbed.
- **Mission:** to rediscover the lost art of tree climbing.
- **Time:** hard to gauge – anything from 10 minutes to several hours, depending on the perseverance – and success – of the unit.

MISSION KEY
£ £ £ £ £   JT   AT

KIT LIST:
- Trainers.
- Basic first-aid kit.

Set expectations. Climbing trees is a wonderful experience and will start to help your troopers appreciate nature and the great outdoors. However, failure while climbing a tree is also important. Trial and error is the best teacher, encourage your trooper to dust themselves off and keep going. Victory will be so much the sweeter!

INSTRUCTIONS:

Your troopers can:

1. **Select a tree.** Trees are nature's climbing frames and come in all shapes and sizes. If your troopers are new to climbing trees, go for trees that have low, thick branches and perhaps gnarly roots for them to get a good foothold. It's OK to start with a big tree as your troopers can stay in the low branches until they gain confidence.

2. **Select a route.** Encourage troops to try to work out their route before they start to climb as this will help them to learn how to read a tree from the start. If they are confident to swing on the lower branches, this will not only help to build their confidence but also test the strength of the branches before climbing them. For the first few climbs you stay at the bottom of the tree as the troops are more than likely to need advice about where to put their hands and feet to get up – and down – the tree.

3. **Climb.** Technique will come with time. In the beginning troops will scramble up the tree in the best way they can, and this should be encouraged. The object of the exercise is to climb a tree, not to be concerned about how they appear to others.

Tree climbing is addictive. If you and the unit see a great climbing tree, make a mental note of its location and head back there when circumstances permit.

MISSION ACCOMPLISHED

I verify that on this date .... I climbed to new heights with my Commando Dad.

Signed: ....

MAKE A ROPE SWING

Mission brief

- **Ground:** woods, or garden if you have a suitable tree.
- **Situation:** a large, strong tree with a clear area at its base (so those on the rope can swing without coming into contact with anything) and a branch at least 16 cm thick.
- **Mission:** to make – and use – a rope swing. If you are on private land, seek permission from the landowner to a) be there, and b) construct a rope swing.
- **Time:** 30–40 minutes once you have everything you need. This does not include time spent reporting back to the stores for some kit, or completing a recce of the area to select the best tree.

MISSION KEY: CONSTRUCTION £££££ JT AT

MISSION KEY: SWINGING £££££ JT AT

KIT LIST:

- Laid rope, at least 2.5 cm thick.
- String or cord to help get the rope over the branch.
- A counterweight to help get the string or cord over the branch. A padlock is ideal.
- Gaffer or electrical tape to cap the cut end of the rope.
- A log/small branch if you'd like to incorporate a seat. This must be small enough to sit on comfortably, while being thick enough to support the heaviest person's weight.

WARNING

It's vital you carry out your Trooper Boundary Brief for this mission. Please exercise caution, common sense and close supervision to ensure troopers are a safe distance away when you throw the counterweight into the tree, and are subsequently able to enjoy their rope swing without hurting themselves unnecessarily. Bumps, scrapes and bruises are par for the course, but bad sprains and breaks must be avoided.

INSTRUCTIONS:

For instructions on how to tie the knots used in this activity – with the exception of the double constrictor knot – see *'Mission 3: Knots' in Adventures in Base Camp.*

1. **Recce.** If possible, find the best tree before you set out on the mission. This will enable you to get directly to the task in hand when your troops are there, and also you will be able to gauge the length of the rope you'll need and cut it back at base camp.

2. **Tie a bowline towards the end of your rope.** (For instructions on how to tie a bowline, refer back to the *'Mission 3: Knots' in Adventures in Base Camp.*) This is a sturdy and reliable knot that will eventually secure the rope swing to the branch.

3. **NB –** If you want to strip out your swing later on, make sure to attach a double length of string through your bowline loop while it is at ground level. By pulling on these strings, you will be able to loosen off the loop when it is at the top and draw the rope down again to take it off the branch.

4. **Put a figure-of-eight stopper knot underneath** the bowline to ensure it doesn't come undone.

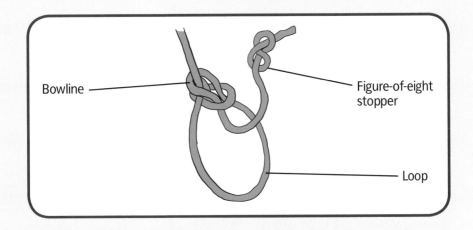

Bowline

Figure-of-eight stopper

Loop

5 **Wrap gaffer tape around the end of the rope to prevent fraying.**

6 **Get your rope swing over the chosen branch:** at the other end of the rope (the one without knots), attach the string or cord to the counterweight with a simple overhand knot (see diagram below). You can secure the knot further with more gaffer tape. Throw your counterweight over the branch so that it takes the rope around the branch and down to you. You can now remove the counterweight.

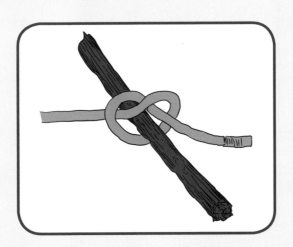

7 **Thread the end of the rope without knots through the bowline.** This will form a loop. Then pull, and keep pulling until the loop is tight around the branch above.

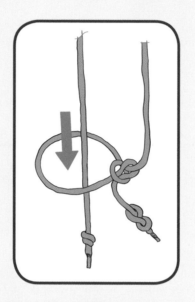

8 You now have a basic swing. **Make two big overhand knots** in the bottom of the rope to create 'riding turns' which you can stand or sit on, and **wrap gaffer tape around the end of the rope to prevent fraying**.

9 **Construct a seat.** If you'd like a seat, fasten a suitable piece of wood to the rope with a double constrictor knot, a simple and secure binding knot.

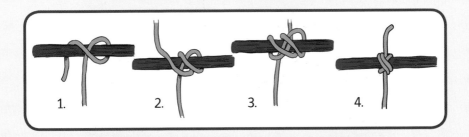

1. 2. 3. 4.

- Wrap the rope around your piece of wood with an overhand action, bringing the working part of the rope left over the standing part, and halfway over the piece of wood again (*see step 1 above*).

- Bring the working end the rest of the way around the piece of wood (*see step 2*), and wrap it over and under again, to make a an 'X' shape with a double line on one side. Then thread the working end under the two loops and up through the top part of the 'X' shape (see step 3). Pull the working end and standing part to tighten and you have your constrictor knot (step 4).

- Use your gaffer or electrical tape to cap the end of your rope to finish it off, so it doesn't fray.

10 **Test your swing** – a task for Commando Dad – sit on the swing seat (without swinging at first) to ensure all knots are holding. Once you are satisfied that your swing is safe, just confirm that there are no previously unseen obstacles that could get in the way when you swing.

11 **Swing!**

MISSION ACCOMPLISHED

I verify that on this date .... I made a rope swing with my Commando Dad.

Signed: ....

MISSION 19:
PLAY CONKERS

Mission brief
- **Ground:** any.
- **Situation:** autumn.
- **Mission:** to play conkers.
- **Time:** anything from 10 minutes upwards.

MISSION KEY

👣👣👣👣👣 £££££ JT AT

KIT LIST:

- Fully locked and loaded conkers, complete with string
  (*see 'Mission 43: Identify a champion conker' in Adventures
  in the Making* for advice on how to prepare your conker).

INSTRUCTIONS:

The aim of the game of conkers is to break your opponent's conker – or horse chestnut.

1 **Take your positions:** players face each other, far enough away to avoid being hit in the face by fast-moving conkers.

2 **Decide who goes first.** A coin toss is usually deemed fair.

3 **Wrap the conker string around your hand:** the player whose conker is getting struck should wrap the string around their hand several times, and let the conker hang down. Conkers must be kept perfectly still.

4 **The first player to strike** is able to determine how high the other player holds their conker. They then swing their conker down hard to strike the other player's.

5 The game continues until one of the conkers is smashed off its lace.

THE RULES OF PLAYING CONKERS

- If a player intentionally moves their conker, the striker gets two shots.
- If the strings tangle, the first player to call 'Strings!' gets an extra shot.
- If a striker hits a conker so hard it goes round in a full circle – known as a 'round the world' – then they get an extra shot.
- If a player drops their conker or has it knocked out of their hand by the striker then the striker can shout, 'Stamps!' and jump on it, but only if the conker owner hasn't already shouted, 'No stamps!'

Badges of honour

A conker can be named to advertise its battling prowess. A new conker is a *none-er* meaning that it hasn't won any conker battles. It becomes a *one-er* after its first success, then a *two-er*, *three-er*, etc.

MISSION ACCOMPLISHED

I verify that on this date .... I conquered conkers with my Commando Dad.

Signed: ....

MISSION 20:
PLAY HIDE-AND-SEEK, COMMANDO-STYLE
(SARDINES WITH A TWIST)

Mission brief

- **Ground:** can be anywhere, but be careful if you are in a wood. We don't want hide-and-seek to become search-and-rescue.
- **Situation:** best avoid weather where the hiders or seekers can be tracked by their opponents (when it's snowing or muddy, for example).
- **Mission:** to get back to base camp undetected.
- **Time:** will happily engage players for an hour at least.

MISSION KEY

£ £ £ £ £   JT   AT

KIT LIST:

- Players (the more the better).

Note: If the players really want to improve their chances of not being detected, see how they can camouflage themselves in *'Mission 28: Cam up'* in *Adventures in the Great Outdoors.*

This is a good activity when entertaining larger numbers of troopers from other units.

INSTRUCTIONS:

1 **Choose a seeker and a base** (it's best if the base is in a clearing if you are playing in woods). Don't forget your Trooper Boundary Brief.

2 The seeker closes their eyes, then **counts to 20 slowly while the rest of the players hide**. Twenty is a good number because players must remain within earshot for the game to be effective and the relatively short time encourages them to hide nearby.

3 Once they get to 20, the seeker must leave the base. **All hiders must stay exactly where they are.**

4 When the seeker finds their first hider, they shout, 'Two's up!' meaning there are now two seekers. **The seekers can choose whether to stay close together** or set off in different directions.

This is the cue for all other hiders to get back to base camp before being detected or caught by an ever-growing number of seekers.

5 **Every time a seeker finds another hider they must shout out the number** ('Three's up!' 'Four's up!', etc.).

6 **If a hider breaks cover and runs for base, as long as they can get there without being touched by a seeker, they are safe. They then must shout 'One safe at base!'** (and subsequently 'Two safe at base!', etc.) so that everyone in the game can keep count of how many are safe, how many are seeking and how many are still hiding.

The first one back at base is the ultimate winner, and they can either choose to be the seeker in the next game or nominate another player.

7 **If any troopers get into any sort of trouble or difficulty, they should very loudly shout, 'End-ex!'** This will alert both Commando Dad and everyone else that someone is in need of assistance.

MISSION ACCOMPLISHED

I verify that on this date .... I learned valuable lessons about hiding and seeking with my Commando Dad.

Signed: ....

MISSION 21:
COMPLETE A SCAVENGER HUNT

Mission brief

- **Ground:** woods.
- **Situation:** any – you can adjust the hunt to match the season.
- **Mission:** to identify key objects and experiences in the environment.
- **Time:** this is determined by you. On average six to ten items will take an hour. Be aware that you will need to either research or recce the woods beforehand to know what is available.

MISSION KEY

£££££ JT AT

KIT LIST:

- A scavenger list (make your own, or use the spot-it sheet on p.116–117).

- Plastic punched pockets (one per player), which will make the list weatherproof and serve as a place to keep items.

- Pencils (one per player), as they will work in all weathers and temperatures.

- Antibacterial hand gel, just in case.

Make sure your troops are given a Trooper Boundary Brief, and know beforehand not to eat any berries or fungi they may find on their scavenger hunt. If you know about foraging and want to include it in your scavenger hunt, please make sure you check with the landowner beforehand, as it may not be permitted.

INSTRUCTIONS:

1 **Make the scavenger list.** Once you know what you are likely to find in the woods, given the time of year and the terrain, you can start to put together a list. Make sure your list includes a mixture of activities, as this is more engaging than just having to find things. So, for example:

- **Items to find and keep:** these need to be put in their plastic pocket, so make sure they're light, small enough to carry and pretty tough. These should <u>never</u> have to be picked; they should be items you can readily find on the forest floor:
  - Acorns.
  - Pine cones.
  - A pine needle.
  - Specific leaves (make sure you provide a drawing if they're not familiar with the shape).
  - A sycamore seed (a helicopter).

- **Items to find and record:** these items your troopers can sketch, on the same paper as their list. Again, you'll need to have done your research, if you include tracks:
  - Deer tracks.
  - Rabbit tracks or poo (a favourite).
  - Badger tracks.
  - Fox tracks.
  - Rough bark (they can make a rubbing of this).

- **Items to experience:** these really encourage the troops to pay attention to what is going on in the environment around them. I don't record these, we just experience them together. But it is possible to record sounds or take pictures on your phone, if you wanted a more permanent memento:
  - Listen to the wind high in the trees.
  - Listen to birdsong.
  - Smell wild garlic.
  - Feel the bark on three different trees.
  - Crunch through fallen leaves.

2 Deploy troopers in your chosen area, ensuring you have a visual on each one at all times.

SCAVENGER HUNT 'SPOT IT' SHEET

Acorn ☐

Pine cone ☐

Pine needle ☐

Leaf ☐

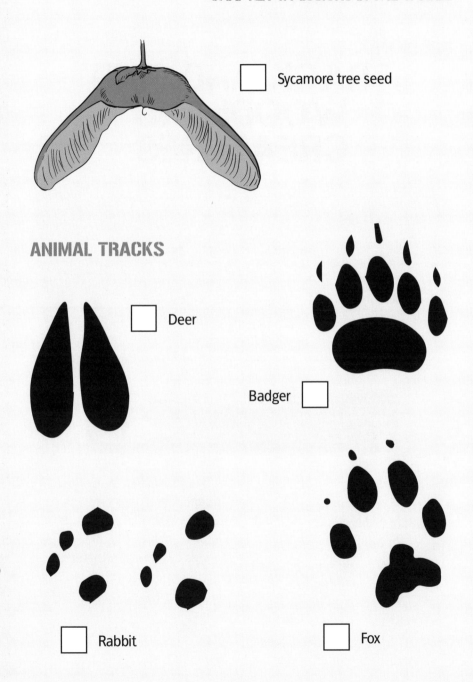

Sycamore tree seed

ANIMAL TRACKS

Deer

Badger

Rabbit

Fox

TRACK AND FIND WOODLAND CREATURES

Mission brief
- **Ground:** woods.
- **Situation:** winter is especially useful as there is less foliage to hide tracks, etc.
- **Mission:** to track the diverse wildlife in our woodland.
- **Time:** this will be determined by you. Allow at least an hour for this activity.

MISSION KEY

£ £ £ £ £   JT   AT

KIT LIST:

- A camera or smartphone, if you want to record finds.
- A chart that shows the wildlife you're likely to find in the UK. They will help prepare the troopers, and again later when troops are reviewing their photos/pictures. You can find great downloadable 'spotting sheets' for UK wildlife – or the resources to help your troopers make their own – at www.wildlifewatch.org.uk/spotting-sheets. They are helpfully sorted by season and habitat.

- Binoculars, if you have them. Troops love them.
- Antibacterial hand gel, just in case.

Set clear expectation here. Woodland creatures are elusive, practised in concealing themselves and expert at avoiding their top predator: people. This means that the unit may track the signs of them all day but not catch a glimpse.

INSTRUCTIONS:

1 **Decide how serious you want to be.** If you want to track wildlife, you'll need to be quiet, camouflaged (not cammed up, nor in very bright clothes that make it even easier to be spotted by wildlife) and probably in the woods very early in the morning, or at dusk. If this is something your troops are interested in, then you will want to follow as many of the steps below in an attempt to track – and hopefully find – the animal you're looking for.

However, if your troopers don't have the patience, inclination or time to track animals, it can still be a great adventure to follow some of the steps and look for the clues below. Older troopers may also enjoy using a camera to capture what they find.

2 **Do your research** so you know what to look for, and where. Pick your day and route carefully. If you go to an area popular with dog walkers for example, you're even less likely to see any woodland animals. Make sure to add birds to your list, as even if woodland mammals prove elusive you'll normally be able to spot a bird or two.

3 **Walk into the breeze** to avoid animals catching your smell. If you have found something you want to monitor (for example, a badger sett – in which case you'd need to be there around sunset), climb a tree to lessen your scent.

4 **Be silent.** If you need to talk, whisper. You might want to agree on a code beforehand – no sudden movements though – such as:

- Index finger to lips (silence).
- Hold your fist up, palm side facing outward (stop).
- Index and middle finger of one hand to each of the eyes and then point with the same hand (look in that direction).
- Touching the top of the head with the fingers ('on me' or 'come to me').

5 **Think like the animal you're tracking.** This will help you work out where you're most likely to find them. For example, the main diet of a badger is earthworms, which favour grassy fields. Woods are a good place to start looking for badger tracks and setts. Deer eat bark and so look for trees where the bark has fresh vertical marks from a recent meal.

Blue tit

6 **Look for footprints.** This is especially effective in winter because plants will have died back, which makes tracks in mud especially easy to find. Tracks also show up well in snow.

7 **Look for homes.** Many woodland animals build their homes in the ground:

- Badger sett: most likely on sloping ground, with a wide hole at the opening. Fresh piles of earth around the sett mean that it is in use.
- Rabbit warrens: most likely on slopes or banks. The holes are typically round or oval.
- Wood mice or vole holes: most likely to be under tree roots. Often camouflaged with twigs, earth and stones.
- Rat holes: most likely close to water and under a cover, such as tree roots. Likely to have freshly dug soil outside.

- Water vole holes: very similar to a rat hole in that it is close to the water's edge (and these voles are sometimes known as water rats). They prefer steep-sided earthy banks beside slow-moving water, and their holes are roughly circular.

Water vole

8 **Look for poo.** This will help you figure out the animal's identity. If it's fresh, that means the animal was there recently. There's also some great poo-spotting sheets available online. I guarantee that's one piece of homework no trooper is ever going to complain about.

9 **Look for fur and feathers.** It can sometimes get caught on brambles or fences and will give you a clue about what animals have passed through.

Finding wildlife

If you are lucky enough to be rewarded with spotting wildlife:

- **Stay still:** keep the elation contained and silent or you will simply frighten them away.
- **Observe**: what are they doing? Are they young or old? Unless you are able to take a photo in absolute silence and without taking your eyes off the animal, I would recommend that you just be present for those few precious moments.

MISSION ACCOMPLISHED

I verify that on this date .... I answered the call of the wildlife in Britain with my Commando Dad.

Signed: ....

MISSION 23:
BE AN EXPERT TRACKER

Mission brief

- **Ground:** woods.
- **Situation:** summer.
- **Mission:** to get as close to the target as possible without being spotted.
- **Time:** depending on the patience of the troops, at least an hour.

MISSION KEY

KIT LIST:

- Cammed up troopers (*see 'Mission 28: Cam up' in Adventures in the Great Outdoors).*
- Stopwatch or timer.

INSTRUCTIONS:

1 **Choose a target for the trackers.** I have found for the first round it's normally good if this is Commando Dad.

2 The target stands on an observation point, closes their eyes and counts to 20 slowly while **the rest of the players hide**. Twenty is a good number because you want to keep all trackers relatively nearby.

3 Once they get to 20, the target looks up, **the stopwatch set for 10 minutes starts** and the target begins scanning the area for trackers. They must stay in the same area (to give slow-moving trackers a chance to reach them) but make sure they use everything at their disposal – eyes and ears – to find trackers.

4 **If the target spots a tracker they shout, 'Spotted!' and then walks over and touches them.** That tracker then stands up, and the target returns to their observation point.

5 **If a tracker manages to touch the target,** then they win the game and can either choose to be the target in the next game or nominate another player.

6 **If all trackers have not been spotted at the end of 10 minutes,** the target says, 'End track,' and all trackers must stand. The nearest one to the target wins, and can choose to be the target in the next game or nominate another player.

MISSION ACCOMPLISHED

I verify that on this date .... I learned to track with my Commando Dad.

Signed: ....

BUILD A FIRE

Mission brief

- **Ground:** woodland – check with the landowner if they allow fires to be built in their woodland before you go ahead.
- **Situation:** when you and the unit need warmth and/or a method of cooking.
- **Mission:** to light a fire.
- **Time:** anywhere between 30 minutes and hours.

MISSION KEY

£ £ £ £ £   JT   AT

KIT LIST:

- An ignition source: matches or a lighter are a great place to start. Advanced methods include flint and steel, a fire steel or friction.

- Stones to enclose your fire circle.

- A garden trowel to dig a fire pit (if not using stones).

- Tinder: to catch the initial spark from the ignition source and transfer it to the kindling. If the kindling is damp or wet, the tinder must burn long enough to dry out the kindling. Good sources: dead dry plants and grasses, wood shavings, cotton wool.

- Kindling: needs more bulk than tinder so it can ignite easily, produce sustained heat and flame, and light the main fuel source. Good sources: dry twigs and wood pieces, cardboard.

- Bulky fuel sources for sustained burning. Good sources: dry wood that is 2 cm to 12 cm in diameter, peat, dried animal dung, coal.

WARNING

Please exercise caution, common sense and close supervision throughout every stage of this exercise and give your troopers a Trooper Boundary Brief before you begin. It might be a good idea to practise in the garden back at base camp before venturing out and about.

INSTRUCTIONS:

1 **Clear a circular area about 1.2 m in diameter** (the 'fire circle').

2 **Build a ring of rocks** around the fire circle to insulate the fire (alternatively, dig a fire pit about 15 cm deep with a small garden trowel).

3 **Pile the trooper-collected kindling loosely** in your fire ring or fire pit. The kindling needs to be dense enough to light but spaced out enough to enable air to circulate (fire needs oxygen to burn).

4 **Place the trooper-collected tinder on the pile of kindling. Light the tinder with your ignition source** and gradually add more kindling.

⑤ Slowly blow air on the igniting fire to build heat and intensity.

⑥ When your kindling has 'caught', that is, is burning well, **start adding firewood**.

Start with the smallest sized pieces and work your way up to larger pieces. The arrangement of the firewood determines the fire's longevity, how fast it burns, and how long it lasts. The most effective arrangement is the teepee.

Making a teepee fire

- Arrange the tinder and a few sticks of kindling in the shape of a cone.
- Stick four kindling twigs in the ground to form a teepee above the tinder.
- Leave an opening through which you can light the fire, ideally on the upwind side to ensure any flame will blow up and towards the wood.
- Build up the rest of the teepee, from small kindling twigs to larger twigs to logs, making sure there is room for air to circulate.
- Light the tinder at the centre.
- As the flames become established the outside logs will fall inward and feed the fire.

Putting a fire out safely

If you want to leave the site before the fire has burned out naturally, you will need to put it out and return the area to as close as possible to how you found it. Remember, a Commando Dad adopts a 'leave no trace' attitude when doing any activity in the great outdoors.

- Poke the burning items away from each other.
- Soak the fire with water, or smother with sand.
- When there is no smoke the fire is out.

> For videos on how to build a fire, or safely put a fire out, go to the Mission Adventure section on www.commandodad.com.

MISSION ACCOMPLISHED

I verify that on this date .... I tapped into a primal instinct – to make fire – with my Commando Dad.

Signed: ....

MISSION 25:

TOAST MARSHMALLOWS ON AN OPEN FIRE

Mission brief

- **Ground:** the woods, or your garden.
- **Situation:** around a campfire.
- **Mission:** to toast marshmallows, ideally over a fire you helped create.
- **Time:** an hour + to prep the fire (*see 'Mission 24: Build a fire' above*), then 2–3 minutes per marshmallow for a nice gooey middle.

MISSION KEY

£ £ £ £ £   JT AT

KIT LIST:

- A campfire.

- Marshmallow sticks: wooden skewers used for barbecues, one for each of your unit. They should be at least as long as your forearm. If not, bind two together with gaffer tape.

- Gaffer tape.

- Something to sit on. Toasting marshmallows is a social activity.

- Heavy gardening gloves as a safety precaution in case you need to get anything out of the fire (a job strictly for Commando Dad).

WARNING

This activity includes fire, sticks and potentially molten marshmallows. Please exercise caution, common sense and close supervision throughout the whole task and give your troopers a Trooper Boundary Brief before you begin.

INSTRUCTIONS:

1 **Light your fire** following the *'Mission 24: Build a fire'* instructions above.

2 Allow your fire to **burn down until there are glowing embers,** which could take an hour or so. When you have that, it's time to toast marshmallows.

3 **Set up seating arrangements.** Pull up a log or camping chairs.

4 **Insert your sticks directly through the centre of your marshmallows.** Accuracy is key here to ensure an even toasting on all sides.

5 **Hold your stick a few centimetres above the embers.** Don't allow your marshmallow to touch the embers as they will burn.

6 **Slowly rotate your stick to get an even toast.** It will start to bubble and brown as it cooks.

7 **The outside of the marshmallow should be brown and crispy.** The inside will be gooey and incredibly hot so encourage your troopers to let them cool for a few minutes – and blow on them profusely – before eating them carefully off the stick.

8 **Enjoy and repeat.**

MISSION ACCOMPLISHED

I verify that on this date .... I cooked marshmallows on a campfire made by me and my Commando Dad.

Signed: ....

BUILD A NATURAL LEAN-TO SHELTER

Mission brief

- **Ground:** woods, best around autumn time so you have plenty of leaves.
- **Situation:** calm weather, especially if you intend to sleep out in it.
- **Mission:** to create a natural shelter.
- **Time:** at least 2 hours.

MISSION KEY

£££££ JT AT

KIT LIST:

- Ridge pole: a straight long branch as thick as your forearm. It determines the length of the shelter, so it should be longer than the tallest person in the shelter. It needs to be alive – that is, green and have sap in it – to be strong enough to use.

- Two sturdy trees to rest the ridge pole against. They should be just over the body length of the tallest person apart.

- Two strong forked sticks to hold up the ridge pole, as tall as the chest of the tallest person. Again, these need to be alive.

- Brash (foliage from the woodland floor), longer branches to create the roof, and lots of twigs and branches.

WARNING

You might need to use a saw or a knife to complete this mission. In addition to exercising extreme caution around the troops, please see 'Knives and the Law' to ensure that you understand the law and that you are adhering to it.

INSTRUCTIONS:

Before you start building your shelter, you need to select the right site. So, consider the following:

- **Materials:** for this shelter, choose an area where there are plenty of sticks, poles, leaves and ferns.

- **Comfort:** check the floor for roots and rocks before you start building. Keep away from insect nests. Check to make sure the ground is not wet or liable to flood if it rains heavily.

- **Safety:** look all around for hazards before you start building, including falling trees and pooling water.

1 When you have chosen the best site, place the two forked sticks on the inside of your selected trees.

2 Place the ridge pole between the forks of your sticks, making sure the pole goes BEHIND your selected trees, and protrudes at least 30 cm at each end.

3 Adjust the angle of the forked sticks so that they lean about 45 degrees, and make sure the end of your forked stick is embedded 18 to 20 cm into the ground so that it won't slip. This angle also helps secure your ridge pole in place, and stops any lateral movement.

4 Test the strength of your ridge pole by hanging off its centre. It should hold your weight. If it does, continue. If not, find another ridge pole.

5 The 45-degree angle you've created with your forked sticks gives you the slope of your 'roof', and you're now ready to start creating your waterproof covering.

6 Lean longer sticks and branches against the ridge pole, at about every 30 cm. They must extend about 20–30 cm above the ridge pole. These will act as roof supports.

7 Arrange branches, brash and twigs on top of the roof supports, until the canopy is thick and sturdy. Aim for a depth between fist and elbow deep to ensure it is insulated and waterproof.

8 Starting from the bottom, start laying dead leaves all over the shelter.

9 When you think the outside of the shelter is complete, go and lie in it. If you see any daylight, add more leaves.

10 Prepare your floor:

- Flooring will insulate the unit from the cold ground.
- Make a thick 'mattress' of brash.

The aim is to make the shelter just big enough to accommodate your unit. Making a shelter that's any larger is a waste of time, resources and energy, and any extra space on the inside will also make your shelter colder than it would be if it were a little more snug.

MISSION ACCOMPLISHED

I verify that on this date .... I sheltered with my Commando Dad.

Signed: ....

MISSION 27:
BUILD A TARP SHELTER

Mission brief
- **Ground:** woods – check with the landowner that it's OK to build a shelter in their woods before you go ahead, and whether it's OK to engage in nocturnal missions.
- **Situation:** calm weather, especially if you intend to sleep out in it.
- **Mission:** to create a tarp shelter.
- **Time:** at least 2 hours.

MISSION KEY

👣👣👣👣👣   £££££   JT AT

KIT LIST:

- Tarpaulin (tarp) with grommets (these are reinforced holes that allow you to put up your shelter). Choose the one that's the right size for your unit, bearing in mind the design that you want.

- Paracord, string or twine to attach the tarp to trees. Six to eight lengths, 1 m each, will do the job. It is always better to have longer lengths as you can tie them off to make them the required length.

- Three stakes to attach your shelter to the ground. These need to be about 15 cm long and 3 cm wide, so look for suitable sticks on the ground, or you can use normal tent pegs if you have them.

- Mallet, if you have one, to drive your stakes/tent pegs down. If not, just improvise and use a rock (a task for Commando Dad or ATs).

- Two trees, to anchor the shelter, about 3–5 m apart.

- Brash (foliage on the woodland floor) and lots of twigs and branches.

Before you begin:

- To secure your tarp shelter, you'll need to know three knots:
  - For the fixed end of your ridgeline, you can use a **Siberian hitch.**
  - To tighten the ridgeline, you can use a **trucker's hitch**. This will provide tension to your tarp.
  - For the corners of your tarp, you need an adjustable knot, so you can use a **tautline hitch**.
  - Once you have your knots mastered, go to p.139 to see how to apply them.

Siberian hitch:

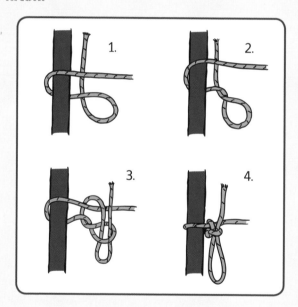

- Swing your rope/cord around the tree, then put the working end under the cord where the load is going to be i.e. under your ridgeline.
- Make a loop in the working end, making sure that the ends going around the tree are parallel (see step 1. in diagram).
- Twist your loop once (see step 2.).

- Make a bight in the working end, bring it over the standing part (ridgeline), then feed it through your loop and tighten.
- To release, simply pull on the working end and the knot will untie.

Trucker's hitch:

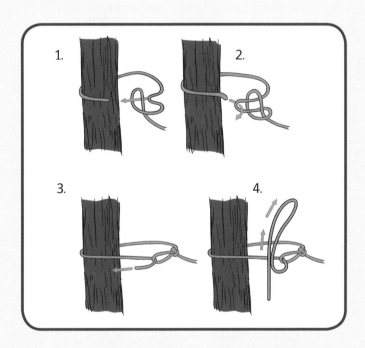

- Swing your rope/cord around your tree, make a loop and hold.
- Bring the standing part towards the tree in a bight, then push it through the loop you've just created. (See step 1. in diagram). Pull the standing part and standing end to pinch the bight and make a loop on your line.
- Feed the working end through the loop you've just created, creating a pulley system. Pull the working end towards the tree to create tension in your ridgeline (see step 3.). Make sure you have at least 20 cm of rope at your working end.

- Once you're happy with the tension in the ridgeline, hold the working end firm. Make a large bight in the working end and drape it over the standing part leading from your loop in the line to the tree (see step 4.).

- Take your working end, make a bight, and pass it under and through the draped bight. Capture the second bight by tightening the line around it. This leaves you with a quick-release option – just pull the working end to release the hitch.

Tautline hitch:

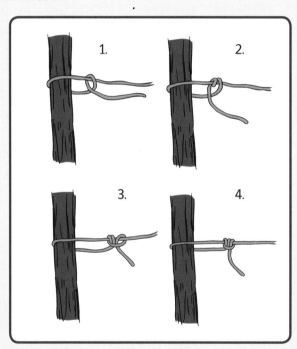

- This is an adjustable knot. One end of the rope will be attached to the tarp, using a round turn and two half hitches.

- Swing your rope/cord around your tree, and put the working end over the cord that is heading towards your tarp.

- Wrap the working end three times around the tarp cord, then bring the cord parallel to the tarp cord.

- Go below and wrap around and through. You can now adjust the knot up and down to adjust tension.

INSTRUCTIONS:

1 Improvisation is the name of the game with tarp shelters. These instructions are for a canopy-type shelter, but you can also make a more traditional A-frame shelter and any number of combinations.

2 Before you start building your shelter, you need to select the right site. So consider the following:

- **Materials:** for this shelter, choose an area with two trees about 3–5 m apart.

- **Comfort:** check the floor for roots and rocks before you start building. These can be really uncomfortable to lie on. Keep away from insect nests. Check to make sure the ground is not wet or liable to flood if it rains heavily.

- **Safety:** look all around for hazards before you start building, including falling trees and pooling water.

> ▶ For videos on how to tie the knots you need to pitch your tarp shelter, go to the 'Mission Adventure' section on www.commandodad.com.

Pitching instructions:

Make the ridgeline or tension your tarp:

- Take two small sticks to help secure your tarp cords to the grommets at either corner of your tarp. This will make sure that pressure is distributed evenly and prevent the grommets from being torn out. You can also use a round turn and two half-hitches to attach your tarp cords to the grommets.

- Using the Siberian hitch, attach one end of the tarp to the first tree, at about shoulder height.

- Using the trucker's hitch, attach the opposite end of the tarp to the opposite tree and tighten. The tighter the tension of your ridgeline or tarp the stronger your shelter will be.

- When that's secure, attach tarp cords to the loose corner grommets and edge grommets of the tarp, using a tautline hitch, and then stake the shelter to the ground.

- Climb under your shelter.

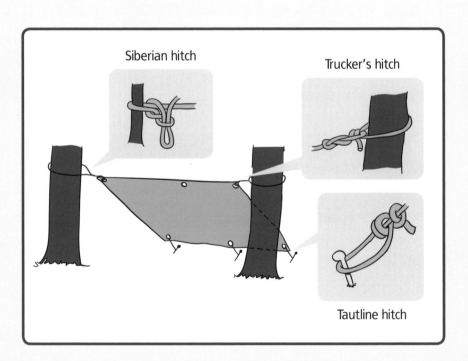

CHECKLIST FOR NOCTURNAL MISSIONS

- The first thing to consider is to get permission from the landowner that it's OK to sleep overnight on their land. This is common courtesy and being a Commando Dad is all about respecting others.
- Shelter and sleeping-out kit. As well as your tarp shelter kit and your Basic Mission Adventure Kit, you'll want kit that is going to keep you comfortable throughout the night, so a roll mat and sleeping bag for each member of your unit is a great idea. You can use blankets, but be prepared for a spot of conflict resolution if you have a blanket hog!
- Toilets. If you are out in the woods, you probably won't have toilets available. Not a problem if all you need is a wee, but poos can be more challenging. Preparation and planning is important here. Consider the age of your troopers and use your Commando Dad common sense to gauge if they are ready for 'open-air pooing'! **DON'T FORGET TO PACK THE LOO ROLL!**
- Water. If you are only planning to stay out for one night, it's best to take water with you. Allow a couple of litres for each person for drinking and cooking. That should be plenty.
- Food. Again, preparation is key here. Once you've decided what to have, do as much prep at base camp as you can, and transport to your overnight camp. For example, if you are planning a stew, chop the onions and carrots at home and carry them in sandwich bags, ready to add when necessary. Remind troopers that keeping hands and eating utensils clean is really important.
- Snacks. It's really important to have high-calorie snacks in your kitbag for your unit. You use a lot of energy when you are out and about adventuring in the woods, so avoid trooper hunger at all costs. Snacks such as banana chips (avoid fresh if at all possible. They tend to 'explode' in your kitbag), dried fruit and trail mix are calorie-rich

foods, but a cheeky bit of chocolate always went down well with my troopers.

- Breaking down your overnight camp – remember, a Commando Dad leaves no trace of ever being in a location, and that is especially true when camping out overnight. Make sure you take away everything that you brought with you, so other adventurers can enjoy the unspoiled woods, just as you have.

MISSION ACCOMPLISHED

I verify that on this date .... I created a tarp shelter, secured with knots and lashings, with my Commando Dad.

Signed: ....

MISSION 28:

CAM UP

MISSION KEY

£ £ £ £ £   JT AT

KIT LIST:

- Cam cream or face paint to disguise the face and hands. You can buy cam cream (which is a type of face paint) at camping or fishing shops, but face paints are just as effective.

- Baby wipes for cleaning up after your mission is complete. Remember, a Commando Dad leaves no trace so take all used wipes away with you.

- Camera to capture how well the unit blended in.

- Dark boots or wellies (which can be edged with foliage). Dark trainers if not.

- Old, battle-hardened clothes that are OK to adventure in.

- A dark coat, with a hood if possible.

- Large, thick elastic bands to attach foliage to the body. Ensure they are not too tight as they will cause discomfort.

- Brash: foliage from the forest floor – select carefully. Avoid spines and stingers.

Good activity when entertaining troopers from other units.

 WARNING

<u>Don't ever</u> use boot polish as cam cream. It is oil-based and will resist all but the most rigorous attempts to remove it.

INSTRUCTIONS:

1 Use a buddy system throughout the task as troopers will need to help each other to succeed.

2 **Make your way into the woods.** Encourage troopers to look around them and take note of the changes they see in the colours of the plants, trees, leaves and the ground.

3 **When it's time to begin, break out the cam cream or face paints.** Buddies put cam cream on each other's faces, ensuring a good covering especially on cheekbones, noses and foreheads. Finish with ears and neck.

NOT ENOUGH   JUST RIGHT   TOO MUCH

④ Troopers put three or four elastic bands around their arms and legs and take it in turns to disguise each other. This involves pushing brash under the bands and keep doing so until the trooper looks like a bush. More elastic bands can be added. Make sure the bands aren't too tight around the arms and legs of your troopers.

Foliage should also be stuffed into boots. It's important that the trooper should still be able to move around – not least because their next task is to disguise their buddy.

⑤ Time to test your camouflage. The most effective way to test your camouflage is to put it into action, with a game such as *'Mission 23: Be an expert tracker'* p.122.

This is a great activity for encouraging teamwork. It also helps the whole unit to pay attention to the environment around them, and to improvise, adapt and overcome to find what they need to blend in.

MISSION ACCOMPLISHED

I verify that on this date .... I learned how to hide in plain sight with my Commando Dad.

Signed: ....

CHAPTER 5:

MISSIONS IN WIDE OPEN SPACES

COMPLETE A TIME TRIAL ASSAULT COURSE

Mission brief

- **Ground:** park, large garden or any wide open space.
- **Situation:** any.
- **Mission:** to get round the assault course as fast as you can. For park-based assault courses, choose a day when the park is likely to be empty (cold or rainy days, for example) to stop innocent victims getting caught in the crossfire.
- **Time:** dependent on the length and complexity of the course. Allow at least an hour for participation, course set-up and break-down.

MISSION KEY

£££££ JT AT

KIT LIST:

- Trainers with a good grip.
- Old, battle-hardened clothes that are OK to adventure in.
- Waterproof notepad.
- Pencil.
- Water to replenish the troops.
- Whistle.

For an improvised assault course:

- Suitable equipment you could carry from base camp: hula hoops, skipping ropes, bats and balls, etc.
- Suitable equipment you can find in the landscape, such as benches, trees, bushes, etc.

INSTRUCTIONS:

1 **Check the course for potential hazards:** broken glass, items hidden in the grass, sharp edges, dog poo, etc.

2 **If using an improvised course, set up the course with your troops.** Obstacles will be dependent on the ability of your troopers and the space available. Here are some ideas to get you started:

- Hula hoop: troopers have to pick up the hula hoop, and do a couple of full spins.
- Skipping rope: troopers can either complete a prescribed set of skips, or it can be laid on the ground for a tightrope walk.
- Commando crawl: troopers have to crawl on their stomachs underneath a tarpaulin or scramble net that's been staked down on the grass.
- Ball skills:
  - Throw a ball/s into a bucket (the balls can be different sizes and the bucket further away for different abilities).
- Physical Training (PT): use the space by having troopers run from A to B, or do cartwheels or forward rolls.

3 **Ensure you have a finish line** for everyone to aim for.

4 **When the course is set up, brief the troops.** Ideally, give them a demonstration yourself and ensure everyone is clear and understands what's expected.

Set the troops off one at a time, while you and the rest of the unit shout encouragement.

5 **Ask a trooper to time you** as you do the course.

6 **Record everyone's time in the notebook.** This gives everyone the opportunity to discover their personal best – and exceed it.

For Park Assault Course:
Find a park with suitable equipment: slides, monkey bars, climbing frames and walls, firemen's poles, etc.

MISSION ACCOMPLISHED

I verify that on this date .... I set a PB (personal best) time on the assault course with my Commando Dad.

Commando Dad's best time: .... My best time: ....

Signed: ....

MISSION 30:
MINESWEEPER

Mission brief

- **Ground:** wide open space.
- **Situation:** flat ground.
- **Mission:** to clear a minefield.
- **Time:** depends on players. Allow 10 minutes to set up, and 5 minutes for each trooper to crawl through.

MISSION KEY

£ £ £ £ £   JT   AT

KIT LIST:

- Old, battle-hardened clothes that are OK to adventure in.

- Mines: I use potatoes, but any soft, smallish object will do, and a bag to put the cleared mines into.

- Marker lines for the minefield: anything is suitable from sticks to discarded clothing.

- Blindfold.

- Stopwatch or timing device.

- Notepad and pencil to record mines disarmed (i.e. brought out of the minefield).

If you have a lot of troopers, divide them into teams and count each member's mines towards the team goal.

INSTRUCTIONS:

1 **Mark out your minefield using** sticks, after carrying out your Commando Dad Safety Check.

2 **Blindfold the first player.**

3 **Scatter the mines** (potatoes) randomly in the minefield. Have one player guide the minesweeper into the minefield. The minesweeper gets on all fours and shouts, 'Ready!'

4 **Start the stopwatch for 5 minutes.** The minesweeper crawls around the minefield while the rest of the team shouts directions, such as 'warmer' and 'colder' for nearing or moving away from the target respectively, or 'forward', 'back', 'left' and 'right'.

5 The clearer should **sweep one hand to feel for mines, and listen to instructions** from the unit. If the minesweeper finds a mine, they pick it up and place it into their mine clearance bag.

6 **With 30 seconds left, the group needs to guide the minesweeper out of the minefield.** If the minesweeper is in the minefield at the end of the round, none of the mines that they've cleared count.

The winner is the trooper with the most number of mines cleared at the end of the game.

At the end of each round, the next minesweeper should be blindfolded, then you can redistribute the mines ready for clearing.

MISSION ACCOMPLISHED

I verify that on this date .... I navigated a minefield with my Commando Dad.

Commando Dad disarmed .... mines. I disarmed .... mines.

Signed: ....

FLY A KITE

Mission brief

- **Ground:** wide open space free from obstacles, such as trees and electricity pylons.
- **Situation:** windy, but no higher than force 6 on the Beaufort scale (*see overleaf*). Absolutely never fly a kite in a storm.
- **Mission:** to fly a kite.
- **Time:** depends on how long both the wind and your troops' enthusiasm holds.

MISSION KEY

£££££ JT AT

KIT LIST:

- Kite (*see 'Mission 42: Make a kite' in Adventures in the Making*).

Set expectations. This activity is completely dependent on the weather, which in the UK is changeable. Kite-flying is improved by skill and experience, but not dependent on it. No wind – or too much wind – means no kite-flying. On kite-flying day, check the weather forecast to see how much wind you can expect.

The Beaufort scale

Force	Description	
0	Calm; smoke rises vertically.	Calm
1	Direction of wind shown by smoke drift, but not by wind vane.	Light Air
2	Wind felt on the face; leaves rustle; ordinary vanes moved.	Light Breeze
3	Leaves and small twigs in constant motion; wind extends light flag.	Gentle Breeze
4	Raises dust and loose paper; small branches are moved.	Moderate Breeze
5	Small in trees in leaf begin to sway; crested wavelets form on inland waters	Fresh Breeze
6	Large branches in motion; whistling heard in telegraph.	Strong Breeze
7	Whole trees in motion; inconvenience felt when walking.	Near Gale
8	Breaks twigs off trees; generally impedes progress.	Gale
9	Slight structural damage occurs (chimney-pots and slates removed).	Severe Gale
10	Seldom experienced inland: trees uprooted; considerable structural damage occurs.	Storm
11	Very rarely experienced; accompanied by widespread damage.	Violent Storm
12		Hurricane

INSTRUCTIONS:

1 Use a buddy system to launch the kite.

2 **Ensure there are no obstacles.** The buddy holds the kite, while the flier steps backwards away from them, unravelling the string from the winder, for about 10 m. The wind should be blowing against the back of the buddy (if the wind is behind the kite it will be pushed down, rather than lifted up).

3 **Launch:**

- The flier signals to the buddy to release the kite; the buddy will then throw it upwards, ideally with a gust of wind behind it.
- The minute the kite is released, the flier should run to improve the chances of the kite catching the wind.
- To make the kite go higher: release more string from the winder.
- To lower the kite: wrap the string around the winder.

4 **Adapt with the wind.**

MISSION ACCOMPLISHED

I verify that on this date .... I scaled great heights with my kite and my Commando Dad.

Signed: ....

MISSION 32:
READ A COMPASS

Mission brief

- **Ground:** any.
- **Situation:** any.
- **Mission:** to learn the basics of compass reading and work out the direction of travel.
- **Time:** an hour.

MISSION KEY

£££££ JT AT

KIT LIST:

- A compass.

Direction of Travel Arrow

Baseplate

Red Orientating Arrow

Compass Bezel/Dial

Magnetic Needle

INSTRUCTIONS:

Before they learn to read the compass, troops must understand its basic layout. The principle is that the compass has a magnetised needle that orients itself to the earth's magnetic field and always points to magnetic north.

Your trooper can:

1 **Hold the compass correctly:** in the outstretched palm of the hand, at chest level.

2 **Work out the direction they're facing** by looking at the magnetic needle (the only part of the compass that moves.) The bezel can also be moved by the Trooper navigating.':

- If the trooper is facing north, everything will line up with the red orientating arrow.
- If the trooper is not facing north, the magnetic needle will be moving to the left or right of the orientating arrow.
- **The magnetic needle always faces magnetic north.**
- The trooper should adjust the bezel of the compass (not their position) until the orientating arrow lines up with the magnetic needle.
- The 'direction of travel' arrow on the compass will indicate the direction your trooper is facing. It may be between two compass points:
  - North and east: northeast.
  - South and east: southeast.
  - South and west: southwest.
  - North and west: northwest.

3 More accurate information can be gathered by **looking at where the direction of travel arrow meets the degree dial**. So, for example, if it intersects at 60, the trooper is facing 60 degrees in that direction (for example, 60 degrees northwest).

Encourage your trooper to move to different places and work out their position, until they are comfortable with reading the compass and its basic layout.

MISSION ACCOMPLISHED

I verify that on this date .... I started to learn compass reading, as a foundation for future explorations with my Commando Dad.

Signed: ....

MISSION 33:
READ A MAP

Mission brief
- **Ground:** great outdoors.
- **Situation:** any.
- **Mission:** to navigate using a map and compass.
- **Time:** at least an hour with compass and map in hand. Be aware that you will need to recce the ground and prepare a route card prior to this activity.

MISSION KEY

£ £ £ £ £   JT   AT

KIT LIST:

- One route map of the area you wish to navigate for every explorer. You can prepare this, or if you're in an area with a visitor's centre you may be able to pick up a local, basic map. Don't start with an OS map as they're too complex and will overload your troopers with too much information.

- One route card for every explorer. Break down the route into stages, each one starting and finishing with a clearly defined feature (this can be anything permanent in the environment, from a rubbish bin to a park bench or tree, for example).

- One pencil for each explorer.

- Compass

Date:		Unit names:		
Stage	**Start point**	**Direction**	**Bearing**	**End point**
Stage 1	Car park	NW	320 degrees	Oak tree
Stage 2				
Stage 3				
Stage 4				
Stage 5				

INSTRUCTIONS:

Before you begin:

Everyone in the unit takes it in turns to be the navigator – to hold and read the compass. With one compass, it is easier for you to make sure it is being read correctly and for the troops to work together.

- Lead the unit to the start point.
- Hand out route maps, route cards and pencils.

- Troopers should fill out the date and their name.
- Choose the first navigator.

1 **Read the compass**:

- Troopers should already be familiar with the basics (*see 'Mission 32: Read a compass'*).
- The first instruction on example route is to go northwest or 320 degrees.
  - Find out on the compass where NW is (or 320 degrees, if your troopers would rather go by bearings).
  - **Turn the bezel** so that northwest on the compass **aligns with the large direction of travel arrow**.
  - Troopers then **turn themselves until the compass needle is aligned with the lines inside the compass housing**.
  - Troopers must **ensure that the red, north part of the compass needle points at north in the compass housing.** If the red part of the needle is facing south instead (it will still look aligned), the unit will head off in the exact opposite direction.

2 **Troopers head off** in the correct direction until they reach the end point on their route card. They can mark the route on the map.

3 **Once a target has been reached,** another trooper becomes the navigator.

MISSION ACCOMPLISHED

I verify that on this date .... I navigated using a map with my Commando Dad.

Signed: ....

CHAPTER 6:

MISSIONS IN WINTER

MISSION 34:
BUILD A SNOW FORT

Mission brief

- **Ground:** wide open space where snow has fallen. The two essential ingredients are snow and space.
- **Situation:** deep, fresh, heavy, undisturbed snow.
- **Mission:** to build a snow fort and repel the enemy.
- **Time:** depends on how big you want your fort to be. The bigger the fort the more time you'll need, but allow at least an hour.

MISSION KEY

£££££ JT AT

KIT LIST:

- A fresh fall of heavy snow.
- Suitable togs for the cold.
- Rectangle containers to make snow blocks. Anything from an empty ice cream tub to a plastic storage box will work, but if the container is too big, the blocks will be too heavy to move around easily.
- Shovel to mark out the fort, fill the containers with snow and smooth down walls. You will need a heavy-duty shovel for the main bulk of the work, but you may want to bring along smaller shovels for the troopers (those used for sandcastles are ideal).
- A small plank of wood to serve as a door lintel (if required).
- Bucket to pour water over your walls to prevent them from melting and for decorative flourishes on walls, if required.
- Water to replenish the troops and to coat the walls (but only if the temperature is below freezing).

INSTRUCTIONS:

1 **Plan your structure.** This can be done at base camp the night before, as the snow falls.

2 **Find a perfect site.** Find a good snowdrift and make sure the snow is dense and not too loose. A snowdrift will mean less work for the unit as the snow is already piled up: you just have to make blocks out of it.

When you get to the chosen site:

- **Measure and mark the size of your fort** (in trooper paces).
- Mark the fort's perimeter with a shovel.
- If there's not been a big drop of snow, opt for a single wall with two wings on either side.
- If you have a huge snowfall, start to execute the perfect structure you planned at base camp.
- **Start making snow blocks.**

3 **Build the snow fort:**

- **Make the walls:** position the snow blocks as straight as possible. The unit needs to work like bricklayers: building the first layer of the wall and stacking the next layer so that each block straddles the blocks beneath. Gaps can be filled with snow 'mortar'.
- Once your walls are at the desired height, add decorative flourishes at will. Using buckets to make castellations, hollowing out small windows, etc.
- If your fort is square and you want to make a door (at the back, obviously), you can leave a space. For budding architects, you can also put in a lintel (a plank of wood laid across the top of the gap at the desired height), upon which snow blocks can be laid as the wall continues to grow.

④ Harden the walls:

- If the temperature is below freezing, you can coat the walls with water (thrown on using your bucket or, if at your base camp, a hose). Beware though, if the temperature is above freezing, this will simply turn the outside of your fort's walls to slush.

MISSION ACCOMPLISHED

I verify that on this date .... I built a mighty snow fort with my Commando Dad.

Signed: ....

MISSION 35:
GO SLEDDING

Mission brief
- **Ground:** snowy, not icy.
- **Situation:** daylight on a suitable slope (*see below*).
- **Mission:** to sled while remaining safe – and warm.
- **Time:** hours.

MISSION KEY

£££££ JT AT

KIT LIST:

- Sled.
- Suitable togs for the cold:
  - Helmet. A winter sports one, if you have it; if not, a bicycle helmet. Wearing one yourself is a sure-fire way to ensure the troops do the same, even if they do complain.
  - Winter clothing. Layers are better than bulky items, and waterproof trousers are better than jeans.
  - No 'flappy' clothes, such as scarves or long hats, which may catch on something as the sled passes. These items could cause an accident.
- Vaseline for lips and noses.
- Sun cream. UV rays will reflect off the surface of the snow.
- Tissues for runny noses.
- Flask of soup or another hot drink to revive the troops, plus KFS (cutlery).

INSTRUCTIONS:

1 Go to the top of a suitable slope.

2 Sled to the bottom.

3 Repeat.

The rules of sledding are nice and simple; however, these tips will ensure sledding success for the whole unit:

GOLDEN RULES FOR SUCCESS ON THE SLOPES

Do:

- Find a hill with a gentle slope and a flat area at the bottom that will allow you to come to a gradual stop.
- Sled during the day and when you can see right to the bottom of the slope. You can make sure the coast is clear before setting off and you'll be able to see where you are going.
- Make sure there's enough snow – a fine dusting will give a bumpy uncomfortable ride and you'll probably not make it to the bottom of the hill.
- **Take time for refs and breaks**: to avoid getting too cold and recharge with soup.
- **Be aware of sledding traffic:** that is, other sledders. Once you've come to a stop, move out the way of other sledders and don't walk back up the slope into oncoming traffic. Move to the side of the slope and climb back up that way.

Don't:

- Sled down a very steep slope or one that ends near a hazard: a road, river, lake, tree.
- Sled in icy conditions as the ground will be very hard.
- Sled on a hill with obstacles (trees, for example) unless you have steering and the ability to use it effectively.
- Slide down head first _ever_, even if you're using a helmet.

MISSION ACCOMPLISHED

I verify that on this date .... I conquered a snowy peak with my Commando Dad.

Signed: ....

MAKE THE PERFECT SNOWBALL

Mission brief

- **Ground:** any. The more space the better for actual fighting, but make sure the area is clear of civilians. We don't want any collateral damage.
- **Situation:** dense heavy snow.
- **Mission:** to create snowballs.
- **Time:** depends on the stash – at least 40 minutes.

MISSION KEY

£££££   JT   AT

KIT LIST:

- Snow.
- Suitable togs for the cold: hats, gloves, coats, boots. Layers are better than bulky items, and waterproof trousers are better than jeans.

You may want to engage in target practice back at base camp before any foray onto the battlefield.

INSTRUCTIONS:

1 **Use dense, heavy snow.** Light powdery snow won't pack, whereas wet snow will be slushy which means they will really compact down to become very hard and hurt when they hit.

2 **Wear gloves, not mittens.** You'll need finger dexterity to make – and accurately throw – snowballs.

3 **Make snowballs.** Put both gloved hands into the snow and bring them together, gathering a small mound. Scoop up the pile with cupped hands, pressing firmly with the entire hand; then continue to firm as you round it to a nice, round, aerodynamic shape. This will ensure it does not break mid-balling. (If you squeeze alone in the initial structuring, the centre will collapse and you'll end up with two halves.) The snowball is ready when you feel resistance.

4 **Build an ammo pile.** This is especially useful if you are fighting from within your snow fort (*see 'Mission 34: Build a snow fort'*). You can fire snowballs in rapid succession at the enemy, while they are still trying to make a single snowball to retaliate. Pitiful.

MISSION ACCOMPLISHED

I verify that on this date .... I made a perfect snowball with my Commando Dad.

Signed: ....

CHAPTER 7:

MISSIONS AT THE BEACH

MISSION 37:
EXPLORE ROCK POOLS

Mission brief

- **Ground:** beach, dry and calm weather (May–September are typically the best months).
- **Situation:** low tide, when rock pools will be exposed.
- **Mission:** to find and explore rock pools, and leave them as you found them.
- **Time:** at least 1 hour, and depending on what you see, possibly more.

MISSION KEY

£ £ £ £ £   JT   AT

KIT LIST:

- Wellies or old trainers with a good grip (to keep feet dry and troopers safe while clambering on slippery rocks).

- Clear buckets or plastic tubs, which will allow animals to be viewed from all angles.

- Magnifying glass, if you have one.

- Sun hat and sun cream, if a sunny day.

- Camera, if you want a memento (no finds are to be taken back to base camp).

The pools with the best wildlife are going to be those nearest the sea. Start there, moving up the beach as the tide comes in.

⚠ WARNING

When adventuring at the beach, take all of the normal precautions: find out about the beach you're going to before you visit, check the tide times and follow the advice on local hazard signs. Please always exercise great caution when near the water with your troopers, especially if they are unable to swim. Always watch out where you're stepping in case the rocks are slippery. An older trooper could be a valuable pathfinder if you have one in the unit. If you see someone in trouble in the sea, alert the lifeguard. If there is no lifeguard, call 999 or 112 and ask for the Coastguard.

INSTRUCTIONS:

 Do your research. This is essential to make sure you know where to go, what to look for and when. There is an awful lot of wildlife in a rock pool, and it will vary widely depending on the environment: rocky coastlines, shingle or sand beaches, for example. Take a guide, or take photographs so that you can compare them later. These creatures are quite common:

- Fish:
  - The blenny is common, but it will often be hiding. It's scaleless and dun-coloured – olive-green, grey and brown.
  - The butterfish is also a hider but easier to spot as it looks like an eel. It can actually grow quite long (over 20 cm) and has dark markings on its yellowish skin.

- Prawns and shrimps.
- Starfish.
- Crabs:
  - Beware of the velvet swimming crab – easily identifiable by its red eyes. It's capable of giving a nasty nip. And it will.
- Molluscs, barnacles and anemones:
  - Look for a beadlet anemone, which will look like a small red flower. No one should touch it though, as it's possible to damage its soft body.

RULES TO AVOID DAMAGING THE ROCK POOL

Do:

- Leave animals where you find them.
- Replace any rocks you may have removed, as they're providing valuable shelter to rock pool inhabitants.
- Change the water in your bucket often, so that the water doesn't heat up and harm any creatures you may have in your bucket.
- Leave attached seaweed in place.

Don't:

- Take any creatures away from their habitat. If you put them in your bucket, this is a temporary measure to enable you to look at them up close.
- Use a net as this can damage rock pool inhabitants. Use hands instead, or your clear container.
- Fill your tub with creatures as they may fight.

ROCK POOL 'SPOT IT' SHEET

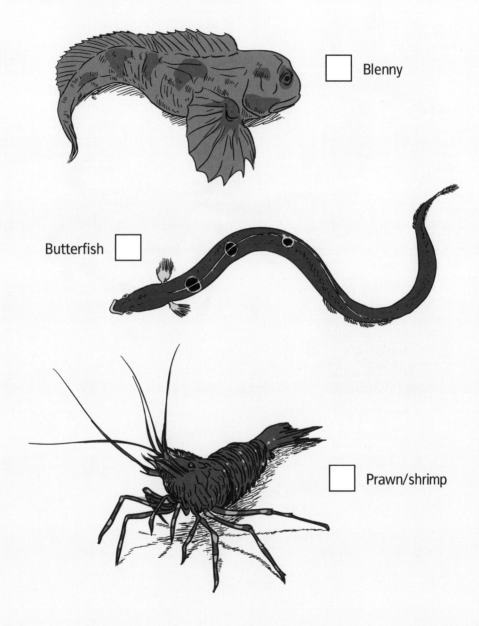

Blenny

Butterfish

Prawn/shrimp

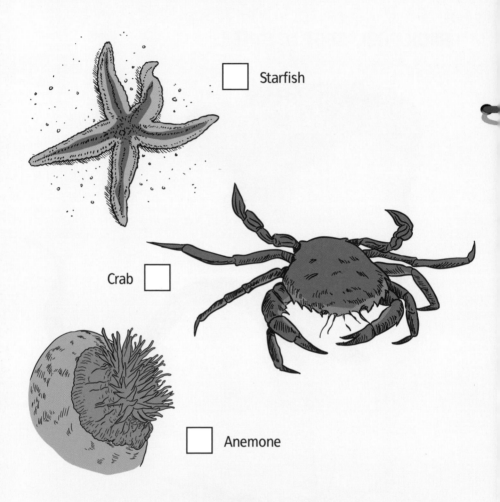

☐ Starfish

Crab ☐

☐ Anemone

MISSION ACCOMPLISHED

I verify that on this date .... I discovered more about the wildlife that lives in the sea with my Commando Dad.

Signed: ....

BUILD AN IMPENETRABLE SANDCASTLE WITH MOAT

Mission brief

- **Ground:** sandy beach.
- **Situation:** a sunny day.
- **Mission:** to create a perfect sandcastle.
- **Time:** anything from 30 minutes. The natural end to a sandcastle expedition is normally an approaching tide.

MISSION KEY

£££££ JT AT

KIT LIST:

- Buckets: the bigger the better. Not only for making castles but also fetching water.

- Spades: the bigger the better. Sandcastle building is serious work.

- Sun hat and sun cream, if a sunny day.

- If you want artistic flourishes, the following will prove invaluable: straws, plastic spoons, melon baller, silicon spatula, palette knife.

- Camera, if you want a memento (no finds are to be taken back to base camp).

WARNING

When adventuring at the beach, take all of the normal precautions: find out about the beach you're going to before you visit, check the tide times (especially important for castle building) and follow the advice on local hazard signs. Please always exercise great caution when near the water with your troopers, especially if they are unable to swim. If you see someone in trouble in the sea, alert the lifeguard. If there is no lifeguard, call 999 or 112 and ask for the Coastguard.

INSTRUCTIONS:

1 **Plan your structure.** This can be a great activity that can be carried out at base camp before departure or on arrival at the beach. Find a handy stick and draw your plan in the sand.

2 **Mark out the perimeter of the sandcastle with your spade.**

3 **Dig out the perimeter (now the moat),** using all available excavation tools: buckets, hands, spades. Throw the sand spoil into the <u>inside</u> of the structure. This will make the platform for your sandcastle, giving it impressive height and also drainage.

When the moat is complete smooth the outside of the sand pile you've made. Leave a dip in the middle.

4 **Add water.** You'll need water to make a castle: only wet sand will stick together and mould into the desired shape. Give your sandcastle a firm foundation of wet sand by adding bucketfuls of water, tamping it down with sand and repeating, until the 'dip' you left is filled in. The wet sand can be tamped down with spades or bare feet (the latter is quicker).

When the platform is complete, fill your buckets with wet sand and start to make your structure, using the biggest buckets first.

When you have an impressive structure, you can decorate as you see fit. Use the tools from base camp to carve out patterns, windows and doors. Use driftwood, shells and other treasures from the beach in the time-honoured fashion.

Take a photo. Structures that come from the sea must return to the sea!

MISSION ACCOMPLISHED

I verify that on this date .... I built a superb sandcastle with my Commando Dad.

Signed: ....

CHAPTER 8:

MISSIONS AT RIVERS AND LAKES

MISSION 39:
BUILD A RAFT

Mission brief

- **Ground:** can be prepared at base camp.
- **Situation:** sunny day at a shallow stream.
- **Mission:** to create a mini raft that floats on water.
- **Time:** allow at least 30 minutes.

MISSION KEY

£££££ JT AT

KIT LIST:

- Large straight twigs.
- String.
- Knife or scissors.
- Pencil.
- PVA or wood glue.

WARNING

Please always exercise great caution when near water with your troopers, especially if they are unable to swim. These instructions also include using a knife or scissors to cut string. Please exercise common sense and close supervision if you intend to let your troopers undertake this task.

INSTRUCTIONS:

Your troopers can:

1 **Gather straight twigs.** Bumps will give you a holey raft, so aim for the straightest ones you can find.

2 Snap them into roughly the same length – **about 20–30-cm lengths**.

3 **Put a stick horizontally in front of you and lay a twig on top of it at one end.**

4 Tie **an overhand knot** around the first twig (see *'Mission 3: Knots' in Adventures at Base Camp*) and then continue to **loop** the string around each twig in a cross fashion (see diagram), **finishing off with another overhand knot**.

5 **Repeat** on the opposite edge.

6 **Secure the knots** by gluing a wooden stick over the top (both sides). Allow to dry.

Troopers write their names on the sticks to identify which raft belongs to whom.

7 **Race your rafts:**

- Find a suitable launch point in the stream: all troopers need to be able to walk easily through the stream.
- Place the rafts in the stream and let the current take them.
- Determine a point for the end of the race.
- The first raft there wins.
- Any dispute over raft ownership can be resolved by reading the names on the sticks.

MISSION ACCOMPLISHED

I verify that on this date .... I sailed a raft across the rapids with my Commando Dad.

Signed: ....

MISSION 40:
SKIM STONES
(INCLUDING HOW TO FIND THE PERFECT STONE)

Mission brief

- **Ground:** rivers, lakes or reservoirs.
- **Situation:** calm, still water with dexterous and patient troopers.
- **Mission:** to skim stones so that they bounce over the surface of the water.
- **Time:** at least 20–30 minutes, depending on the success of the skimmers involved.

MISSION KEY

KIT LIST:

- Skimming stones: light, flat and able to fit comfortably between the skimmers thumb and index finger. The smoother the better (to reduce water drag).

- Bucket: only if you prefer to gather the stones first.

WARNING

Please always exercise great caution when near water with your troopers, especially if they are unable to swim.

Set expectations. It can take a lot of trial and error to perfect a technique. Some never manage! It's also possible to have the right stone, the right position, the right force... and still not get it right. But mastering skimming stones is worth it, as it never fails to impress.

INSTRUCTIONS:

1 **Take the skimmer:** and place it between your thumb and index finger.

2 **Get into position:**

- Face the water side on.
- Get as low as possible as you want to be throwing the stone horizontally across the water, not into it.
- Take your arm back.
- Making sure you keep the flat angle, draw your wrist back.
- Bring your arm forward quickly with as much power as you can muster and then just before you release the stone, flick your wrist forward so the stone leaves your hand, flat and fast.

- Finish with a strong follow-through.

3 **Count the bounces.**

MISSION ACCOMPLISHED

I verify that on this date .... I started to learn the skill of making stones bounce across the surface of water with my Commando Dad.

Signed: ....

MISSION 41:
BUILD A DAM

Mission brief

- **Ground:** shallow stream.
- **Situation:** ideally where water flow is already constricted by an obstacle (a bend or a tree stump, for example).
- **Mission:** to build an effective dam using natural resources.
- **Time:** at least 30 minutes.

MISSION KEY

£££££ JT AT

KIT LIST:

- Whatever is suitable in the vicinity to make a dam: rocks, stones, branches, twigs, logs, brash.
- Camera, if you want a lasting memento.

Good problem-solving exercise.

⚠️ **WARNING**

Please always exercise great caution when near water with your troopers, especially if they are unable to swim. These instructions also include gathering wood and stones. Please exercise common sense and close supervision to ensure troopers are able to carry their dam-building supplies without hurting themselves.

INSTRUCTIONS:

 Find a suitable point in the stream. All troopers need to be able to walk easily through the stream.

② **Forage around the local vicinity for dam-making equipment.** There are only three rules:

- It has to already be on the ground (so no stripping branches off trees, etc.).

- You can use things you've brought with you, but they must be suitable for being in the water (a water bottle full of river water is permitted, for example).

- If you're using something that another, more careless, unit has left behind, it has to be taken back to base camp to be recycled.

3 **Build the dam from the bottom up**, just as beavers do. Larger items, such as rocks and branches, go at the bottom of the structure and can be cemented in with mud if your troopers are willing! Twigs, smaller stones and brash can be used to build up the structure.

   Once the dam is complete, you may choose to see how long it holds.

4 When you've finished for the day, the troops need to **break the dam down** again and make sure all man-made materials are removed and the water can flow freely again.

MISSION ACCOMPLISHED

I verify that on this date .... I stemmed the flow of a mighty body of water with my Commando Dad.

Signed: ....

SECTION 4:

ADVENTURES IN THE MAKING

MISSION 42:
MAKE A KITE

Mission brief

- **Ground:** base camp.
- **Situation:** before windy weather hits.
- **Mission:** to create a classic diamond-shaped kite.
- **Time:** 30 minutes maximum, once you have equipment squared away. Note that you may need to report to the stores for some of the required kit.

MISSION KEY

👣👣👣👣👣 £££££ JT AT

KIT LIST:

- Flying line. You can buy kite line online, or use some other light synthetic thread; for example, fishing line will be suitable.

- Winder. Can be bought online, or in specialist kite shops. You can also make one out of a small block of wood or stiff cardboard.

- Sail. Heavy-duty plastic bags, such as those for garden waste. Ideally, they should be 0.5 m wide and 1 m long.

- Framework. Thin hardwood dowel, around 5 mm in diameter, and to fit the dimension of the sail material which can be found in most DIY shops.

- Electrical insulation tape.

- A ruler.

- Scissors.

- A black marker.

- A small wood saw or a carving knife to cut the dowel.

WARNING

These instructions include using scissors and a small knife for cutting the dowel (which can be quite fiddly). Please exercise caution, common sense and close supervision if you intend to let your trooper undertake these tasks.

INSTRUCTIONS:

1 **Make the sail:**

- Put the bag flat on the floor, with the closed end at the top.

- Starting from just below the top-left corner of the bag, measure and mark three dots on the plastic (*see diagram*).

- Connect the dots using the ruler and marker pen.

- Turn the bag over and trace over all the black lines.

- Cut along the top <u>and</u> right side of the bag.

- Open it out to show the complete sail outline.

- Take your scissors and cut along all the black lines.

- Open the plastic and you'll have a recognisable diamond kite shape.

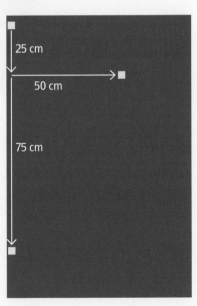

25 cm

50 cm

75 cm

2 **Add the frame:**

- Lay a length of your dowel down the centre of the sail, aligning one end with what will be the top of your sail.

- Cut off the excess dowelling that goes beyond the bottom of your sail.

- Cut 5 cm of insulated tape, and secure down the dowel to the sail at the top and bottom of your kite.

- Repeat this process with the dowel that goes across the kite, left to right.

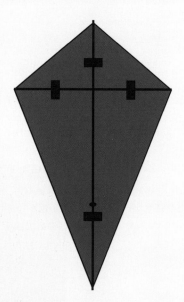

3 **Attach the line:**

- Turn the kite over and, using the very tips of the scissors, poke a small hole in the plastic where the two dowels cross.

- Thread one end of your line through the hole and firmly tie it to both pieces of wood.

- Cover the knot with more insulation tape to firmly secure it.

- Tie the other end of the line to a winder, a small wooden block or piece of board that you can hold comfortably.

4 **Make a cardboard winder:**

- Take a strip of stiff cardboard long enough for your trooper to hold with both hands.
- Cut a slit in the centre, on both sides, without cutting all the way through.
- Put the end of the thread in one of the slits so that it doesn't move as you wind the thread around.

5 **Make a tail:**

- Using scraps of the plastic bag, cut a long, narrow strip at least five times the length of the kite itself, about 5 cm wide.
- Thread one end of the tail around the bottom of your kite's vertical dowel.
- Tie the tail to the dowel with a simple knot.

You are now ready to try *'Mission 31: Fly a kite'* in the Missions in Wide Open Spaces section of this book. If you and your trooper would like to try your hand at making different kites, you can try www.my-best-kite.com for straightforward step-by-step instructions.

MISSION ACCOMPLISHED

I verify that on this date .... I created my own kite with my Commando Dad.

Signed: ....

IDENTIFY A CHAMPION CONKER (AND GET IT ON THE LACE)

Mission brief

- **Ground:** great outdoors.
- **Situation:** beneath horse chestnut trees around mid to late September.
- **Mission:** to take a humble horse chestnut and help it realise its potential for conker mastery.
- **Time:** finding the right horse chestnut is a matter of luck and time cannot be measured. Preparing the conker and getting it on the lace can be achieved within 30 minutes.

MISSION KEY

£££££   JT   AT

KIT LIST:

- Horse chestnuts.
- Plastic bag/tub (for collection).
- Washing up bowl or bucket of water (for selection).
- Newspaper (for protection).
- A meat skewer or Phillips-head screwdriver.
- 30 cm of string per conker.
- Sticky tape.
- 120 ml vinegar.
- A jug.

> **WARNING**
>
> These instructions include using a skewer or thin screwdriver for boring holes in conkers, and this activity should only be undertaken by a Commando Dad.

Conkers get much harder with age so make sure troopers keep their champions for next season. A forward-thinking unit can store some for the following year. Just make sure you bore a hole in them first – no need for vinegar. Ageing will do the work.

INSTRUCTIONS:

Hardening conkers is the stuff of folklore and you may have your own method of gaining a tactical advantage. Here's the one that worked for me as a trooper:

1 **Gather conkers** to take back to base camp.

2 **Break open the prickly green cases** and look for conkers that are:

- Uncracked.
- Firm.
- Symmetrical.

3 Take your selected conkers and **drop them in the bowl or bucket of water**. If they float they have some damage inside and unfortunately do not have the potential to become champions. Discard.

Take your 'sinkers' and put them through their paces:

- Pour the vinegar into a jug.
- Drop your conkers in.
- Leave to soak.

4 Twenty-four hours later, **remove the conkers from the vinegar and leave them to dry** on a newspaper on the kitchen counter.

5 When dry, **bore a hole through each** using a meat skewer or a thin screwdriver.

Take your string and wrap a piece of sticky tape around the end (like you see on a shoelace), as this will help with threading.

6 **Thread your piece of string through the conker and tie in a knot.**

MISSION ACCOMPLISHED

I verify that on this date .... I created champion conkers with my Commando Dad.

Signed: ....

MISSION 44:
MAKE A TEMPLATE FOR TYING KNOTS

Mission brief

- **Ground:** base camp.
- **Situation:** any.
- **Mission:** to create a portable knot tying template to enable troopers to practise and perfect four knots: overhead knot, figure-of-eight knot, reef knot, the bowline.
- **Time:** less than 30 minutes to construct, will be used for hours.

MISSION KEY

£ £ £ £ £   JT   AT

KIT LIST:

- Stiff cardboard 28 x 21 cm (approx.).
- 2.5 m of cord in a single colour.
- Scissors.
- Pencil.
- Ruler.
- Marker pen.
- Phillips-head screwdriver.

NB – this template does not include the knots for building a camp as referenced in Missions in the Woods. That's because those knots involve lashing the tarpaulin to a tree and need to be practised in the field.

WARNING

These instructions include using a screwdriver for making holes in stiff cardboard, and this activity should only be undertaken by a Commando Dad. It also involves cutting cord with scissors so please exercise caution, common sense and close supervision if you intend to let your trooper undertake this task.

INSTRUCTIONS:

1 **Measure twice and cut once.**
   On the back of the card:

- Draw three vertical lines at 7-cm intervals, dividing your card into four columns.
- Draw two horizontal lines at 7-cm intervals, dividing your card into three rows.

You now have 12 boxes.

- The first row is for labels.
- The second row is for the knots, tied correctly as an example.
- The third row is for the practice cord.

2 In the first three boxes on the second and third rows, **mark out a hole in the dead centre**.

3 In the final box on the second and third row **mark out two holes in the centre** of the box, about 3 cm apart.
   When you have the marks in the right place, go over the pencil mark with the marker.

4 **Create the holes.** Place the cardboard on a flat surface and use the Phillips-head screwdriver to push and twist through. Lift it to finish off so that you can push the screwdriver all the way through. Repeat on the other side of the card, for all ten holes.

Overhand knot	Figure-of-eight knot	Bowline	Reef/square knot
◯	◯	◯	◯ ◯
◯	◯	◯	◯ ◯

5 **Create the knots.** Cut the cord into eight roughly equal lengths. Thread a length through the holes, securing at the back with a stopper knot, apart from the last box where the lengths of cord fall at the front of the template.

On the middle row, tie the following knots correctly (see *'Mission 3: Knots' in Missions in Base Camp*):

- The overhand knot – single hole.
- The figure-of-eight knot – single hole.
- The bowline – single hole.
- The reef knot – two holes.

6 Your knot tying template is now ready to be deployed.

For a more permanent template solution, you could use a thin board and a drill, but I find the method described here makes for a more collaborative activity.

MISSION ACCOMPLISHED

I verify that on this date .... I began to learn that practice makes perfect with my Commando Dad.

Signed: ....

MISSION 45:
TAKE FINGERPRINTS

Mission brief

- **Ground:** base camp.
- **Situation:** near soap and water, to ensure the fingerprints stay where they're supposed to.
- **Mission:** to learn to make, find and understand fingerprints.
- **Time:** for all stages, up to an hour.

MISSION KEY

£ £ £ £ £   JT   AT

KIT LIST:

Taking fingerprints:

- Charcoal stick or pencil, ideally a HB (hard black) or B (black) grade.
- Paper to use as your 'ink pad'.
- Light-coloured paper or card to display prints.
- Sticky tape.

Dusting for fingerprints

- A glass.

- Soft brush – a make-up brush is ideal.
- A teaspoon of flour or cocoa powder.
- Small bowl.
- A drop of oil.
- Light-coloured paper or card to display prints.
- Sticky tape.

INSTRUCTIONS:
Taking fingerprints:

Your trooper can:

1 **Make the ink pad.** Take the charcoal stick or pencil and scribble on a piece of paper until they've made a very black mark. It only needs to be about a couple of centimetres square.

2 **Make a fingerprint.** Rub their index finger or thumb on the mark.

3 **Take a fingerprint.** Place a piece of sticky tape over their finger, press down on a flat surface and then peel it off gently.

4 **Reveal the fingerprints** by sticking the sticky tape to the card.

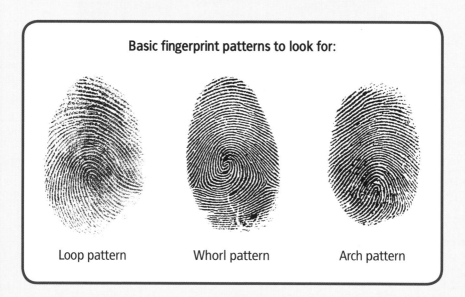

Basic fingerprint patterns to look for:

Loop pattern   Whorl pattern   Arch pattern

Dusting for prints:

Your trooper can:

1. **Put a teaspoon** of powder into the bowl.

2. **Rub a couple of drops** of oil into their fingers. They need to be 'just eaten crisps' oily.

3. **Press an oily finger** on a clean glass.

4. **Load the dusting brush** by dropping its bristles into the powder. Do not overload the brush (excess can be removed by tapping the handle on the side of the bowl).

5. **Gently pass the powder over the surface of the glass.** The fingerprint will become visible as the powder catches the oil.

6. **Remove the print** by placing the sticky tape on the dusted fingerprint. Press down on a flat surface and then peel it off gently.

7. **Stick the tape to light-coloured construction paper** to inspect the fingerprint more closely.

If you have several troopers at base camp, you might want to get them to leave their fingerprints on identical glasses, mix them up and get them dusted for prints. Then see if they can identify whose prints are whose by comparing the dusted prints with the original fingerprint cards they made.

For troopers serious about fingerprints, the US Scouts provide a free downloadable 'Fingerprint Card' based on the one used by the FBI. Troops can fill in their personal details and print it out before adding their fingerprints: usscouts.org/mb/docs/Fingerprinting-Card.pdf.

MISSION ACCOMPLISHED

I verify that on this date .... I had my first foray into the world of forensic science with my Commando Dad.

Signed: ....

MISSION 46:
MAKE A CATAPULT

Mission brief

- **Ground:** the great outdoors, but if the wood is fresh, it will need to be dried out at base camp.
- **Situation:** a controlled environment and, if outdoors, a day with clear visibility.
- **Mission:** to create a catapult and practise shooting accuracy.
- **Time:** once you have everything assembled, less than half an hour. Note that you may need to report to the stores for some of the required kit, and you may need to dry the wood out.

MISSION KEY

KIT LIST:

- Catapult frame, usually a small tree branch with a V-shaped fork that can fit in the hand comfortably. The 'V' shape must be wide enough to have ammo pass through – at least 30 degrees.
- Elastic bands. Latex rubber surgical tubing is best, as it is readily available online and it won't snap. You can buy these complete with pouches online too. Look for 'latex catapult rubber band'.
- If drying the wood:
  - Microwave.
  - Kitchen roll.
  - Plastic bag.
- Dental floss.
- Saw for cutting small branches.
- Knife for making notches and cutting narrow latex tubing.
- Empty tin cans (for target practice).

WARNING

If you want to use your catapult for target practice, then you might choose to use stones as ammo. In this instance, close supervision by you is essential. <u>Never</u> let your trooper fire at another trooper or you – but this is especially true when using stones. Remember the story of David and Goliath? The catapult was even recognised as a deadly weapon in the ancient world – Romans had a special type of pinchers that could remove an embedded stone fired from a catapult from the bodies of soldiers. Even if you have a pair of these to hand, exercise extreme caution.

INSTRUCTIONS:
Build your catapult:

1. **Find your catapult frame.** I advocate finding one on the ground rather than cutting it off a tree. It can be hard to know if it's the right shape for you without holding it in your hand, making foraging the best option. However, if you need to cut one from a tree, look for low-hanging branches and use a suitable saw to cut it safely from the tree.

2. **Ensure your catapult frame is dry.** Wood needs to be dry and rigid for an effective catapult. If your wood has been cut directly from the tree, or not been on the ground long, it will still have sap in it. You can either take the wood back to base camp and store it for later, or dry it yourself. The quickest method is to use a microwave:

- Wipe the frame with a dry cloth or kitchen roll.
- Wrap it in clean kitchen roll and place in a plastic bag but do not seal it completely. The bag will not only help you gauge when the moisture has disappeared but also protect your microwave – and future meals – from odd tastes and smells.

- On high, microwave your frame for 30 seconds and take it out and unwrap it. Let it cool for 10 minutes, then rewrap and repeat. Replace the kitchen roll when it gets too damp and wipe out any moisture from the inside of the plastic bag.

- Repeat until there is no moisture. You will be able to tell this in a number of ways: no hissing and no new moisture on the paper towel.

3 **Carve notches.** You need to carve a notch around the top of each branch of your V to ensure your elastic fits snugly.

4 **Cut the elastics.** There is an art to this. It needs to be long enough to draw back but not so long that it loses power. Cut elastics with a knife.

5 **Attach the elastics** by sliding the end of the tube through the notches in the V's of your branches, then a little way down the front side of the catapult. Secure with dental floss, which has very strong properties. Tie it as tight as you can and cut the loose ends.

Target practice:

Use clean tin cans for target practice as they're a good size and weight, and make a gratifying sound when you hit them. Make sure you don't place tin cans in front of anything breakable as the ammo can easily ricochet.

Suitable ammo:

In and around base camp:

- Marshmallows.
- Ping pong balls.
- Dry sponge.
- Soft balls.

Great outdoors:

- Acorns.
- Conkers.
- Pebbles and stones (but only under close supervision from Commando Dad).

Ammo in base camp needs to be soft and light. My daughter is still a crack shot with small cuddly toys. When using heavier ammo in the great outdoors, make sure your trooper understands that they are in charge of their catapult at all times and be sure to give a Trooper Boundary Brief. Make it clear that absolutely NO negligent discharge will be tolerated.

MISSION ACCOMPLISHED

I verify that on this date .... I started a journey to becoming a crack shot with my Commando Dad.

Signed: ....

MISSION 47:
MAKE A SLING

Mission brief

- **Ground:** anywhere.
- **Situation:** to be mastered before it is needed in an emergency first-aid situation.
- **Mission:** to master a key first-aid skill: making a sling.
- **Time:** once mastered, a sling can be made in a couple of minutes.

MISSION KEY

£££££   JT   AT

KIT LIST:

- A triangle bandage:
  - To practise, you can use any triangle of material, but try to get a piece without too much 'give' as it will allow the arm to move.
  - The triangle should be about 1 m long, but err on the side of larger (you can adjust it to fit).
- A 'patient'.
- A chair.

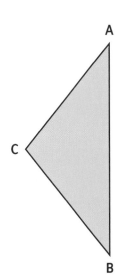

INSTRUCTIONS:

1 **Ask the patient to sit** in the chair and gently hold their injured arm, cradled in their non-injured arm if they need extra support.

2 **Pass the bandage** *gently* **behind the injured arm**.

Bring the top point (A) over the shoulder of the injured arm. The bottom point of the long edge (B) will fall over the hip on the side of the non-injured arm. The third point (C) will fall at the elbow of the injured arm.

3 **Pass (A) gently around the back of the neck to the opposite shoulder (that of the non-injured arm)**. If more bandage is needed, return (A) to its original position and pull gently.
   Bring (B) up to meet (A) at the shoulder of the non-injured arm, making a recognisable sling shape.

If being used to support the injured arm, the patient's non-injured hand will now be inside the bandage, and they need to remove it and cradle their arm from outside the bandage. If they need help, your trooper can hold (A) and (B) together in one hand (keeping the tension) and use their free hand to help the patient.

4 Tie (A) and (B) together at the collar bone using a reef or square knot (*see 'Mission 3: Knots' in Adventures in Base Camp*). (C) now holds the hand of the injured arm.

5 **Make sure the whole arm is supported,** right down to the little finger of the injured hand.

Now fold in the excess by taking the bandage from the elbow across to (C) and twisting it until it fits around the elbow.

6 Tuck in the twisted bandage.

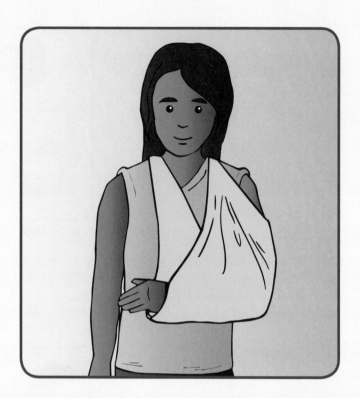

MISSION ACCOMPLISHED

I verify that on this date .... I began to master first-aid skills with my Commando Dad.

Signed: ....

GLOSSARY OF COMMANDO DAD: MISSION ADVENTURE TERMS

Admin: Any jobs or tasks you need to complete to ensure the smooth running of a mission.

Advanced Trooper (AT): This is a trooper between the ages of 9 and 12.

Base camp: Home.

Basic Mission Adventure Kit: A bag of essentials for safe and efficient adventuring.

Buddy system: Where troopers work together to complete a task. A good example is camming each other up – very tricky to do on your own.

Cam up: Where a trooper covers themselves with foliage (branches, leaves, etc.) so they can blend into the background.

Commando Dad Safety Check: Any situation that requires Commando Dad to make sure a mission is safe for his troopers to undertake.

End-ex: Troopers shout this if at any point during a mission they find themselves in any sort of difficulty and need help.

End point: Ultimate destination.

Junior Trooper (JT): This is a trooper between the ages of 5 and 9.

KFS: Knife, fork, spoon; cutlery.

Leave no trace: A Commando Dad wants to have as little impact on an area they visit as possible.

Light-order missions: Short sorties, such as visiting the shops, on the way to school, etc.

Mid-term deployment: Extended times away from base camp, such as long car or train journeys, or flights.

Mini-beast: The insects, reptiles/amphibians, birds and mammals living in your garden.

Nocturnal missions: Any activity that happens after 'lights out'.

Premature detonation: When a water bomb goes off in the hand of the thrower rather than hitting a target.

Physical Training (PT): Any activity that gets your and your troopers' hearts racing.

Recce: Short for reconnaissance, a mission to obtain information.

Refs: Refreshment break.

Sortie: The dispatch of the unit; used to describe a trip away from base camp.

Squared away: Everything organised and in the right place and ready for an adventure.

Squabbling squaddies situation: Possible argument between troopers.

Stand by: This is an instruction for Commando Dad to prepare himself for something: verbal comments, incoming water bombs, etc.

Trooper Boundary Brief: Instructions for troopers on places or things that are out of bounds during a mission.

Unit: Family. Includes your own children and those you care for, partners and other carers.

Up to speed: Where all relevant information, and the mission and actions to carry out, are clear.

Yomping: A long, active walk.

USEFUL RESOURCES

Natural Bushcraft is a UK-based website and forum where you can learn skills from others, and share your own experiences: www.naturalbushcraft.co.uk.

For glow-in-the-dark invisible ink, here is a great website: www.kidsplayandcreate.com/homemade-invisible-ink-and-glow-in-the-dark-messages-recipes-for-kids/

To find your nearest wood, go to the Woodland Trust website: www.woodlandtrust.org.uk/visiting-woods/. You'll also be able to find a wealth of resources including activities to encourage your unit to visit woods, plant trees and treasure our British wildlife.

For a Poo ID sheet, check out this website: www.woodlandtrust.org.uk/naturedetectives/activities/2015/09/poo-id/

Basic first aid is a key life skill. You can find more first-aid activities, straightforward videos, important information and a free first-aid guide (hard copy or download) on the St John's Ambulance website: www.sja.org.uk

---

 KNIVES AND THE LAW

Activities in Section 3: Adventures in the Great Outdoors may require you to use a saw or a knife. In these circumstances, the knife is a tool and should be treated as such. As with any other potentially dangerous tool, it should only be handled by you. If you have limited or no experience of using knives for outdoor crafts, make sure you understand how to use it safely when you buy it. Make sure you know the right knives to use in the right situation. For advice on the safe use of knives, you can ask the shop assistant when you purchase your knife, or ideally, sign up for a bushcraft course, where they will teach you all you need to know about knife safety.

Of course, knives are also considered weapons and there are laws about buying, carrying and using them in the UK. For an overview and more information, please go to: www.gov.uk/buying-carrying-knives. This is the definitive guide and should be adhered to.

The Criminal Justice Act (1988) says that you may carry a knife with a blade length of 7.62 cm (3 inches), but it must fold and not lock. Absolutely **no** fixed blades are allowed.

If you wish or need to carry a larger knife then you need a 'reasonable cause'. That means that you must be able to prove that you had a genuine reason for carrying the knife. A 'reasonable cause' can constitute a whole host of scenarios such as:

- Knives are part of your job (such as a butcher or a chef) and you are taking them to and from work.
- It is associated with sport, such as fishing.

If you are unsure, contact your local police for advice.

The maximum penalty for an adult carrying a knife in public without good cause is 4 years in prison and a fine of £5,000.

Never forget that you have a knife when travelling to and from your destination – and do all you can to make it as inaccessible as possible. When travelling by car, leave it in the boot. When on foot, have it in the bottom of your rucksack.

ACKNOWLEDGEMENTS

The author would like to thank:

- Wildlife Watch, the junior branch of the Wildlife Trust: www.wildlifewatch.org.uk
- The Woodland Trust: www.woodlandtrust.org.uk
- Natural Bushcraft: Ashley Cawley, www.naturalbushcraft.co.uk
- My Best Kite: Nick Parish, www.my-best-kite.com
- Nick Waldock, for sharing all the books and swinging the lamp.

NEIL SINCLAIR

COMMANDO DAD

BASIC TRAINING

HOW TO BE AN ELITE DAD OR CARER

THE BASICS

- Survive the first 24 hours
- Prepare and plan to prevent poor parental performance
- Maintain morale
- Feed, clothe, transport and entertain your troops

FROM BIRTH TO 3 YEARS

Foreword by Dr Jan Mager-Jones MB ChB

COMMANDO DAD

COMMANDO DAD: Basic Training

How to Be an Elite Dad or Carer

Neil Sinclair

£10.99
Paperback
ISBN: 978-1-84953-261-7

ATTENTION!

In your hand is an indispensable training manual for new recruits to fatherhood. Written by ex-Commando and dad of three, Neil Sinclair, this manual will teach you, in no-nonsense terms, how to:

- Plan for your baby trooper's arrival
- Prepare nutritious food for your unit
- Deal with hostilities in the ranks
- Maintain morale and keep the troops entertained

And much, much more.

LET TRAINING COMMENCE!

POCKET COMMANDO DAD:
Basic Training
Advice For New Recruits to Fatherhood

Neil Sinclair

£7.99
Paperback
ISBN: 978-1-84953-555-7

ATTENTION!

In your hand is an indispensable pocket-sized training manual for new dads. Written by ex-Commando and father of three, Neil Sinclair, this no-nonsense guide will teach you how to:

- Prepare base camp for your baby trooper's arrival
- Survive the first 24 hours
- Establish feeding/sleeping routines

And much, much more.

LET TRAINING COMMENCE!

Have you enjoyed this book?
If so, why not write a review on your favourite website?

If you're interested in finding out more about our books, find us on Facebook
at **Summersdale Publishers** and follow us on Twitter at **@Summersdale**.

Thanks very much for buying this Summersdale book.

www.summersdale.com